WHAT OTHERS ARE SAYING ABOUT DAVE AND ASHLEY WILLIS

"Dave and Ashley Willis are so honest and transparent in their writings. I absorb so much from their work and will apply their teachings to my marriage, always."

—**Brandi Rhodes**
Professional Wrestler, Actress, and Lifestyle blogger

"Dave and Ashley's ministry has benefited me greatly. They strive to apply God's truth in an uncompromising and yet grace-based manner. If I see they're behind it, I know it's worth my time hearing what they have to say. I know I'll be challenged, inspired, and motivated to keep Jesus at the center of my marriage."

—**Gary Thomas**
Bestselling author of *Sacred Marriage* and *Cherish*

"Dave and Ashley are some of the best marriage communicators out there. They are funny, relatable, and skilled in sharing biblical truth in a way that will help your marriage for years to come."

—**Ryan and Selena Frederick**
Authors of *Fierce Marriage* and Hosts of *The Fierce Marriage Podcast*

"Dave and Ashley Willis' wisdom has helped countless numbers of people, including me, grow in our personal life, family, and spiritual lives."

—**Dr. Marty Baker**
Lead Pastor of Stevens Creek Church and Founder of SecureGive.com

"Dave and Ashley (or Davo & Ash as we Aussies call them!) have a gift... They both are amazing storytellers and present Biblical truths in a clear and understandable manner. Their books, articles, and podcasts are informative, laced with humor and include some wonderfully embarrassing stories. Their message is GOLD for marriages around the world."

—Andrew "Robbo" Robinson

Co-host "Rise & Shine"–Vision Christian Radio (Australia)

NAKED &
HEALTHY

NAKED &
HEALTHY

*Uncover the Lifestyle Your
Mind, Body, Spirit, and
Marriage Need*

DAVE & ASHLEY WILLIS

TABLE OF CONTENTS

INTRODUCTION

*Dear friend, I hope all is well with
you and that you are as healthy in
body as you are strong in spirit.*

3 John 1:2 (NLT)

Ironically, as we write these first words in a book about health, we're both at home sick with COVID-19. Wrestling with relentless symptoms like headaches, backaches, upset stomachs, exhaustion, and no sense of smell or taste, we find ourselves as passionate as ever about the message you're about to read. That's right, not even the coronavirus can keep us from sharing this message with you! Of all the books and resources we have ever created, we believe *Naked and Healthy* might be the most important. It addresses the core issues that can bring true and lasting health to your marriage, while simultaneously bringing health to every other aspect of your life.

At first glance, a book about marriage and health might seem like a peculiar blend of topics, but in our own marriage and our years of doing marriage ministry, we've found that issues related to health impact every aspect of a marriage. When a couple commits to supporting each other "in sickness and in health," both spouses will be at their best emotionally, spiritually, and physically. The marriage will also grow stronger as a result.

The vow "in sickness and in health" is one of the most important promises you've ever made to one another. It means you'll be there for each other in seasons of great physical setbacks, but it's also a proactive promise to promote health in your own life and to encourage healthy habits for your spouse too. When you'll do this for each other—without shaming or judging each other if their progress isn't the same as your own—all aspects of your marriage can thrive as a result.

Your personal health and the health of your marriage are inextricably connected. In the peaks and valleys of our own health journey, and throughout the years we've been doing marriage ministry, we've discovered three simple principles that have become the foundation of this book. These three foundational principles are:

1. **A healthy marriage requires two people who are each committed to their own personal health (mentally, physically, and spiritually).**
2. **Your spouse's health must be a priority for you, and your own health must be a priority for you.**
3. **Your marriage will never be healthier than you are.**

Just as a quick point of clarification about that third principle, you can thrive in your marriage even when you're facing illness, health setbacks, or poor physical shape. It's also possible to be in peak physical condition and still have a marriage that's deteriorating. If visible abs and chiseled muscles were required to have a great marriage, our own marriage would be in big trouble!

We're also not saying a healthy marriage is impossible when one spouse is sick or facing a physical or emotional setback. On the contrary, some of the strongest marriages we've encountered have faced exceptional challenges, and both spouses found ways to support each other through the struggle. What we are saying is that a *commitment* to health is a prerequisite for a healthy marriage. Even when facing unforeseen (or even permanent) health challenges, you both can still have a commitment to health.

Throughout this book, we will be sharing high points and low points from our own marriage and health journey. In addition to our own stories, we'll also share inspiring true stories from couples we've encountered who are living out these principles. Their stories will offer insight into every aspect of marriage and health. This includes facing the challenges of aging, growing together in your faith, supporting each other in debilitating diseases, working through mental health issues, enjoying sex when you don't like your own body, and supporting each other in reaching fitness goals. We're so thankful for the couples who have motivated and inspired us through their own journeys. We expect their testimonies to encourage you as well.

You will notice that we've divided the upcoming chapters into three main sections: *Mental Health, Physical Health,* and *Soul Health.* There's not a separate section for the health of your marriage because marital wisdom will be interwoven into every chapter. The book is designed to help you grow in your own mental, physical, and spiritual health while simultaneously building a healthier marriage.

As one final note, you might be confused by the word "Naked" in the title. If you're familiar with our *Naked Marriage* book and *The Naked Marriage Podcast,* you already know we have a consistent teaching message rooted in the Bible's lessons about the very first married couple. As Scripture describes it, Adam and Eve were "naked and unashamed." The nakedness represented in those passages was not only physical; it was a picture of complete emotional and spiritual intimacy as well.

We believe God wants all married couples to have what we refer to as a "Naked Marriage." It's a safe atmosphere of commitment and intimacy where each spouse knows each other fully and accepts each other completely.

In this book, we're building on that core message. The lessons in *Naked and Healthy* might inspire you to improve the physique of your physical naked body, but more importantly, we hope these lessons will help you experience growth and healing in all aspects of life, faith, and marriage.

Thank you for your commitment to a healthier marriage and a healthier life. We are on this journey with you. We are praying for you and cheering you on as you strive toward greater health in your marriage and in other aspects of your life. We hope the principles, true stories, and Scriptures on these pages will encourage you to keep growing. Let's get started!

MIND

Do not conform to the pattern of this world, but be transformed by the renewing of your mind. Then you will be able to test and approve what God's will is— His good, pleasing and perfect will.

Romans 12:2

CHAPTER 1:

An Unexpected Setback

Ashley

I recently watched an inspiring interview with a young widow who had four children. This woman had just lost her husband, a police officer, in a terrible accident two months prior. I couldn't help but watch while she described her husband's many favorable attributes with tears in her eyes and a smile on her face. But when the interviewer asked her how she was doing these days, this woman's response wasn't at all what I expected. It has forever changed my perspective.

She told the interviewer that she and her four children were doing well because they were living out one of the phrases that her husband frequently said to all of them. She explained that whenever anyone in the family was having trouble, resistant to change, showing too much "attitude," or doubting their ability to do something, her husband would call them by name and succinctly and lovingly tell them, "**You can do hard things.**"

Though extremely simple, I firmly believe these five words have the potential to completely change one's perspective and resolve. In fact, the concept is biblical.

Philippians 4:13 states, *"For I can do everything through Christ, who gives me strength"* (NLT). And one of my very favorite verses, Deuteronomy 31:6 says, *"So be strong and courageous! Do not be afraid and do not panic before them. For the Lord your God will personally go ahead of you. He will neither fail you nor abandon you"* (NLT).

Let's face it: hard things will come our way (John 16:33). How we consistently handle those hard moments in our life often define the very course we take. When we approach tough circumstances with unabashed perseverance, nothing can bring us down. We *can* do hard things. As believers, we must know and believe that God is with us and He will not forsake us, as we learn in Deuteronomy 31:6. We can do hard things.

The journey toward health can be a difficult one, but you can do hard things. No matter what you're facing right now, no matter what barriers are standing in the way of your total health, you and your spouse can do this.

When your marriage is in a slump and you don't want to work at it anymore, you can go to your spouse and find a counselor to help you communicate more effectively, address your issues, and strengthen your marriage. You can do hard things.

When you have been struggling with your weight all your life and have tried and failed at a thousand different diets, don't give up. Find a strategy that works for you. Keep going after it. You can do hard things.

When you've battled a physical ailment or mental health issue for a long time and you feel like you don't have the strength to take another step, keep going. The Lord is with you in the struggle. His power is made perfect through weakness (2 Corinthians 12:9). You can do hard things.

Maybe you are in the same spot as the young widow I descried earlier. You have lost your loved one, and you don't know how you are going to live another day without him or her. Know that your life is not over, friend. God still has great plans for you, and you can do hard things.

Your spouse can do hard things. You both can get healthier mentally, physically, emotionally, and spiritually. It can be a difficult process, but it is so worth it. You may grow tired and weary, but you can lean on one another and encourage each other to keep going.

We must persist. We must never give up. We can do hard things.

There have been many moments throughout our marriage when I have tried to lose weight—especially after having a baby—but I wouldn't see the weight come off as fast as I wanted. I would get so discouraged when I stepped on the scale to find I had only lost a fraction of a pound after following my meal plan to the letter and exercising every day that week. It was so frustrating!

One particular day, I was sulking around the house, and Dave asked me what was wrong. I told him how disappointed I was that my weight-loss journey was such a slow one. I exclaimed, "I only lost a quarter of a pound this week. A quarter of a pound! Can you believe that? I didn't eat any chocolate. I followed the food plan every day. I exercised like crazy. What's the deal?" Dave listened, and when I finished my rant, he smiled, put his hands on my shoulders, and looked into my eyes. He told me that he thought I looked beautiful just as I was, but he knew that it was really important to me to shed a few pounds. He reminded me that every little bit adds up. He said, "What if you lost a quarter of a pound every week for a year? That's a pound a month. Then, you will have lost twelve pounds in a year! That's awesome.

And some weeks, you will lose more than others. Just keep going! You've got this, Sweetie!"

Those were the exact words I needed to hear in that moment. I needed to know that Dave loved me no matter what, but I also really needed to know that I had his support and that he believed I could lose the weight. He helped me get out of my slump and get motivated. He raved about the healthy meals I made for the family, even though he may have preferred something else. He walked with me regularly at night, even though he had already exercised that day. He cheered me on with each fraction of a pound I lost, and little by little, the weight came off. It was hard to keep going at times, but I didn't give up and ended up losing thirty-eight pounds over the course of nine months! I did a hard thing, and you and your spouse can, too.

As spouses, our support and encouragement of one another can help make these hard things much more bearable. Make it your mission to help your spouse keep going through tough challenges. Cheer one another on through every step.

Throughout this book, you're going to be challenged to do hard things. God's calling for our lives is usually on the other side of our comfort zones. We must be willing to embrace some temporary discomfort for the sake of experiencing lasting growth. The temporary discomfort is always worth the permanent growth.

Dave

Ashley and I always try to encourage each other in the moments when one of us is feeling down or defeated. For me, I can be prone to discouragement and sometimes even Ashley's admonishing can't motivate me to embrace the struggle with a healthy attitude. I need to be reminded that "I can do hard things," but life's setbacks can often deal a blow to my mental health and my overall attitude.

Sometimes the biggest blows to our mental and emotional health come in the form of a sucker punch of unexpected bad news. The bad news can be related to the loss of a loved one, a financial setback or a myriad of other factors. For me, one of those setbacks came through an unexpected diagnosis that simultaneously tested my mental health, physical health, spiritual health and the health of our marriage. In many ways, this diagnosis became the catalyst for this book. It all started with a routine trip to the doctor's office.

I've always hated going to doctor's offices. I usually spend a half-hour filling out the same forms I filled out at the last visit and then waiting past my scheduled appointment time just to be weighed and prodded like livestock. Then, I'm told that I need to either lose twenty pounds or grow six inches taller to be at a healthy weight on their demoralizing BMI chart. After the subtle fat-shaming, I'm stuck in another room waiting for the actual doctor to arrive. Once I do see the doctor, he/she goes through their regular litany of questions. They look inside my ears for some reason before abruptly sending me back to the front desk to cover the overpriced co-pay for the whole experience.

Don't get me wrong: I respect the medical profession. My mom was a hospice nurse and her work inspired me as a child. As I'm writing these words, our world is still dealing with the COVID-19 pandemic and healthcare workers are on the frontlines of the battle doing heroic work to keep us safe. I understand why doctors are vital. I've just never personally liked the experience of going to see them. I'm more likely to stay at home and take Advil when I'm feeling sick. Usually, my approach works out fine and the issue resolves itself before I ever have to see a professional.

This approach has worked well for most of my life. I remained relatively healthy with little medical oversight through my twenties and the first half of my thirties. But when I hit my mid-thirties,

I noticed that my body wasn't working quite like it had before. I chalked up this slight decline to the expected physical effects of aging. My wife wisely realized it was something else entirely.

Ashley is the smart one in our relationship and over the course of the twenty years we've been together, I've learned to trust her instincts even more than my own. Still, my stubbornness gets in the way sometimes. When she started suggesting that I go to a doctor to get some testing done, I resisted. I made every excuse imaginable and told her that I'd make a few tweaks to my diet and "everything would work itself out."

Things got worse instead of better. My energy level was shot, my thinking wasn't clear, my digestive system wasn't working right, and I had a myriad of other issues both big and small. I finally relented and went to the doctor. My routine doctor visit yielded minimal insight into my health challenges, and I was basically prescribed medication to help with digestion.

Over time, the digestion medicine seemed to be doing little to solve the issues. I went to some specialists to have an ultrasound of my stomach and gallbladder. I even considered the possibility that I had contracted a terrible gastrointestinal bug on a mission trip or that I had some kind of intestinal obstruction. I asked a gastroenterologist friend to do an upper endoscopy on me to find what I thought would be the culprit of my health issues. At one point, I was certain they were going to find a giant tumor in my gut because of the pressure I felt there, but they found nothing.

Then the doctors pivoted the diagnosis from digestive-related issues to stress-related issues. I was told that stress was the main factor in all my ailments. This might have been partially true and what ultimately triggered the genetic time bomb of my ultimate diagnosis—we will get to that in just a bit. I was living with a lot of stress, trying to balance family time with four energetic kids plus two different jobs. My pace was unsustainable, and my systematic physical shutdown was possibly my body's way (and God's way) of getting my attention.

I went to see a Christian counselor for therapy, which proved to be incredibly helpful. I highly recommend counseling to anyone who is facing any kind of health or relational challenge. It's healthy to talk through our struggles with someone trained to help us process them. I'm very thankful for that experience and all I gained through it, but my physical symptoms saw very little improvement. There was clearly something wrong inside my body that needed to be identified and resolved.

After at least a year of dead ends with doctors and specialists, Ashley made me an appointment at a new doctor's office. Ashley had visited this office and had a good experience. She encouraged me to give it a try. I reluctantly submitted to her persistent advice and made the appointment.

They ran a wide spectrum of lab tests of my bloodwork, looking for anything at all that could be out of balance. I honestly didn't expect anything to come back from the blood tests. Every other appointment had been a waste of time, and I expected this one to be the same. But when the results came in, I was simultaneously shocked and relieved to finally have some answers.

My doctor explained to me that I had Hashimoto's disease, a form of hypothyroidism. In layman's terms, she explained what hypothyroidism is and how it can be treated. In addition to my thyroid issues, I had a vitamin D deficiency and low testosterone, among some other issues. She explained that all of these other issues might be directly related to the thyroid, and that if we could get the thyroid balanced, the rest of my body would probably get more balanced as a result.

I asked what I needed to do to reach full health and get my thyroid working correctly. In addition to a daily dose of medication—which I'd probably have to take for the rest of my life—she outlined an array of lifestyle adjustments that seemed like they would upend every part of my diet and schedule. In the discouragement of the moment, it felt like a death sentence. While she was incredibly cordial, compassionate and professional, it still felt like she had walked into the room, punched me in the throat and then kicked me in the crotch. I asked her how long I would deal with this. She used the word "lifelong" to describe my condition, which hit me like a knockout blow.

I limped out of the office with my prescription for Synthroid and a library of pamphlets and resources on all the lifestyle changes that would be necessary to combat my thyroid issue. I called Ashley on the way home and calmly tried to explain how we finally had some answers, but we also had a long road ahead. As always, she was incredibly supportive. Hearing her reassuring voice was all I needed in that moment to feel very optimistic about the future.

I started off with an enthusiastic and optimistic game plan, then I went through a little bit of an identity crisis when my diagnosis started sinking in. All this happened when I was thirty-eight years old and I think it might also have triggered a mild midlife crisis. I went from seeing myself as a strong, virile guy in my prime to seeing myself as an aged, frail, tired old man with a "preexisting condition."

Only a few years earlier, I had run a marathon and competed in a strenuous obstacle course "mud run" at a nearby Army base. I'd been serious about physical training and most days I felt pretty invincible. Now, only a few short years later, I'd lost the will to exercise much and felt weak and emasculated.

My low testosterone was part of the problem. Not only was "Low T" a real factor in hurting my strength, energy levels and sex drive, but it also had a psychological effect. Low testosterone can be linked to mental issues such as anxiety and depression, which I was feeling for the first time in my life. I also wrestled with the stigma of seeing my manhood defined by a number—and that number being so low. I would ask myself the vulnerable question, "Am I even a real man anymore?"

These insecurities were exacerbated by well-meaning friends who would learn of my diagnosis and try to relate by saying things like, "Hypothyroidism? Oh yeah, my grandmother has that same thing."

I don't know if it was all in my head, but it seemed like every example I heard of someone who had my same diagnosis was a much older woman. Great! Now, I have no testosterone and an old lady's disease. I might as well be one of the Golden Girls.

I've since learned that while hypothyroidism might be more prevalent in women, it can certainly impact anyone at any age. In those early days after the initial diagnosis, I was just more sensitive than usual. Since my body and mind were still a little out of whack, I was more susceptible to discouraging thoughts, even if those thoughts were baseless and untrue. That was all part of the new reality I was facing. My diagnosis wasn't just a physical issue, but also created mental and emotional issues. Every part of my life was touched in some way.

Ashley's support made a world of difference to me in those early, vulnerable days, and she has continued to be a source of encouragement and perspective for me every day since. She's really the hero of this story. It was her urging and persistence that ultimately led to my diagnosis. It has been her encouragement that has helped me through it. When I was first diagnosed, she responded with such compassion. She prayed with me and patiently listened as I vented and complained. She also helped me laugh. In the early days, she texted me a homemade GIF of Mr. Miyagi from *The Karate Kid* movies saying, "Don't worry, David-san, we will fight Hashimoto together!"

She knows how to get me. I love *The Karate Kid* movies. I love funny GIFs. I love to laugh. While we were facing something serious, it was a beautiful way to remind ourselves that we were not going to lose our sense of humor. In fact, our sense of humor would be one of our most important weapons in the fight ahead.

Being able to laugh helps you reclaim power from something that might have taken power from you. It brings levity and perspective. It's a workout for your abs without having to do crunches or planks. Plus, it just feels good to laugh.

In the days to come, I would experience many more setbacks. But I also experienced incredibly encouraging breakthroughs. Daily, I carried the invisible weight and unseen wounds everyone with an autoimmune disease carries with them. I wish I could go back in time and tell my discouraged self that much better days were ahead. Still, I'm thankful that I walked through those difficult days, because now I'm stronger as a result. I still have a LONG way to go, but I'm finally thankful to be on the journey. I see how God has been working it all together for my good.

Ashley

The road to health always involves doing hard things and this always requires courage. One of the most courageous people in the Bible is a woman named Esther. There's an entire book of the Bible named for her as a tribute to her love and faith in the face of life-threatening circumstances. Her courage defined the fate of a nation.

Esther lived in a time when her nation of Israel had been exiled to Persia under the rule of a king named Xerxes. Esther's beauty caught the king's eye, and after a nationwide beauty contest resembling a super cringeworthy, twisted version of "The Bachelor," King Xerxes chose Esther to be his queen.

The palace insulated Esther from most of the struggles of her countrymen, until her cousin Mordecai informed her that a genocide was being planned against their people. Mordecai told Esther he believed God had put her in a position of influence with the king especially for this time and purpose.

Esther was forced to make a very difficult choice. Although she was the queen, the laws of the land meant she could be executed for entering the king's presence without being invited. Time was short, and she couldn't wait for him to call for her. Still, her decision to approach the king's throne could mean instant death. (King Xerxes could have benefited from some intensive marriage counseling!)

Esther wasn't only willing to sacrifice her life; she was willing to sacrifice her lifestyle. Selfishness could have seduced her into ignoring the cries of her people as she enjoyed the comforts and opulence of palace life. Instead, she refused to remain passive in this fight. Her love for her people proved to be greater than her love for comfort—and even her love for her own life. Esther's heart was so full of love she had no room left for fear.

First, Esther called her people to a time of fasting. They united together in prayer in preparation for her self-invited meeting with the king. When the period of praying and fasting ended, Esther summoned her courage and boldly entered the king's chamber. I'm sure she held her breath as she waited for the king's response.

Fortunately, the king was pleased to see her. Through a series of meetings, Esther eventually was able to leverage her influence to persuade the king to stop the travesty about to take place. She saved her people because she chose to do the hard thing. Her courage changed history, and it was all made possible because of love.

You've probably never had to risk your life the way Esther did, but all of us have had to overcome fears. I don't know what fears in your life have gripped you, but I know that God has the power to loosen that grip. Ask Him to replace any fearful or negative thoughts in your mind with His powerful, affirming truths. Ask Him to give you the strength and grit to do the hard things you need to do. Thank Him for being the ever-present, ever-powerful God that He is. Thank Him for giving you the opportunity to grow healthier in mind, body, and spirit alongside your spouse, and ask Him to strengthen your marriage in the process.

He will do all of these things while sustaining you both in this amazing journey towards a holier, healthier, and happier life and marriage. As you look for practical ways to create healthier habits like the ones we'll discuss in the upcoming chapters, know that you can do this!

You are courageous. You are chosen. You are called.

You can do hard things.

Dave

I've never faced a challenge nearly as daunting or consequential as Esther faced, but I have faced my share of mental, spiritual and physical challenges. One of the most difficult physical challenges I've faced was trying to run a marathon. I use the word "trying" because my first attempt was a brutal failure. It was an unseasonably hot day and I wasn't prepared for the heat or the hills on the course. I ended up exhausted and dehydrated, lying under a bush as I tried to catch my breath.

At that point, a little boy took pity on me and offered me his bicycle so I could make it to the finish line. I didn't take his bike, but I skipped the last five miles of the race and hobbled to the finish line with a broken spirit and a broken body. After some time resting in the medical tent, I reconnected with Ashley and the boys. They had been watching for me at the finish line and I had to tell them that I had not finished the race.

That was a difficult day, but I refused to let that be the final chapter in my marathon story. I realized that I had not properly trained the first time, and without proper preparation, I had set myself up for failure. The next time around I would need disciplined training as well as accountability. I found both in my friend Josh, who is a United States Marine and an elite athlete.

Josh was also training for a marathon and took me under his wing. We scheduled long runs together several times per week, and he would never let me give up. He kept pushing me. In the moment, there were times I hated the accountability, but I also knew it was making me stronger. He also kept it fun. Once I asked him how I could get my leg to stop hurting. With a quick-witted, deadpan response, he said, "All you have to do is open up a can of Man."

I laughed out loud. That phrase, "Open up a can of Man," has been my go-to phrase every time I wanted to quit training because I knew my Marine buddy was right: I needed to "man up" and push through. Once the day of the race arrived, I was ready. I was far from an elite athlete and I knew I wasn't going to finish anywhere close to the front of the pack, but I also knew I was going to *finish*. There were still many moments I wanted to quit along the course, but the training and accountability I'd received during those three months leading up to the race were enough to carry me through the painful miles.

In life and in marriage, there are going to be times you want to quit. There will be times you need to have the faith and resolve to open up a "can of Man" (or "can of Woman") and push through. Offer accountability to your spouse and allow your spouse to do the same for you. Stay prepared in season and out of season by embracing daily disciplines in your health and you'll be equipped for whatever life throws your way. You may never set the goal of running a marathon, but life will put you in many long "races" that require your perseverance. So, finish the race strong! You can do hard things if you'll support each other in hard things.

Ashley

Dave and I have faced our share of fears and unexpected setbacks. Many of these have been related to our health. Recently, we both faced the unexpected setback of being diagnosed with COVID-19. Even as I write these words, we're still at home under quarantine, having experienced symptoms for almost two weeks.

In the midst of a global pandemic, we have joined the millions whose lives have been touched by this illness. We've experienced the uncertainty and anxiety related to fears of worst-case scenarios. We have battled relentless symptoms, which left us both feeling physically and mentally exhausted. We've tried to be strong for each other, even in moments when both of us felt weak and depleted.

In moments like this, we are reminded of God's faithfulness. We are reminded that His power is made perfect in weakness. We are reminded that He will never leave us or forsake us. We are reminded that moments of shared struggles can result in exceptional growth in our faith and in our marriage.

As I write these words, we appear to finally be emerging from the effects of the illness. We are starting to feel like ourselves again, which is a huge answer to prayer. Feeling healthy is a gift most of us take for granted—until an illness or injury leaves us feeling powerless. We are so thankful our health is returning.

In your life and your marriage, you're going to face unexpected setbacks. Perhaps you are in the midst of one right now. Whatever you're facing, face it with the faith of Esther and the strength that comes from knowing God is with you. Face it in partnership with your spouse. You will get through this. You will come out stronger on the other side. God never wastes our pain. He will use this for your good and His glory. Trust Him.

CHAPTER 2:

Anxiety and Depression

Ashley

According to statistics from The Anxiety and Depression Association of America, "Anxiety disorders are the most common mental illness in the U.S., affecting 40 million adults in the United States age 18 and older, or 18% of the population."[1] Anxiety disorders are highly treatable, yet statistics show that only a third of those suffering receive treatment. When left untreated, anxiety can take a tremendous toll on one's marriage and family.

In this chapter, Dave and I will unpack some of the complex issues related to anxiety and depression. If this isn't a struggle you or your spouse are currently facing, you might be tempted to skip over this chapter, but I strongly encourage you to keep reading. Anxiety and depression can sneak up on you even when you think it could never happen to you. Dave and I both know this from personal experience.

I started experiencing anxiety firsthand as a young teen, but I didn't understand it or even know what to call it at the time. That's

1. Anxiety and Depression Association of America, "Facts & Statistics," Anxiety and Depression Association of America, ADAA, https://adaa.org/about-adaa/press-room/facts-statistics.

the funny thing about these mental disorders. We think the experience is normal at first. But when it lingers, we fear that we might be "crazy." We become embarrassed. This keeps us from reaching out to a trusted friend or family member, and we suffer in silence. However, getting help is key in fighting anxiety and/or depression. We will share more about this later in the chapter.

We are all prone to having anxious thoughts from time to time, but a person dealing with anxiety has anxious thoughts that keep coming back, day after day. Those of us who suffer with anxiety feel the weight of these worrisome thoughts piling up in our mind, and they are heavy on our hearts as well. We often have trouble sleeping because these anxious thoughts plague us at night and keep us up. Then there's the possibility of anxiety/panic attacks. Those are a doozy. If you've ever experienced one, you know what I mean.

It usually starts with a fear that you just can't shake. Sometimes, you can't even pinpoint the exact fearful thought at the time, but the feeling of fear and worry overwhelms your mind and body. You start sweating. Your heart beats faster and faster. Your respirations rise, and you feel like you can't breathe in enough oxygen. That only makes you more anxious until you feel a churning in your stomach. Sometimes, you have to run to the bathroom because the churning produces vomit or diarrhea. Your mind races, and you think you might be having a heart attack. You try to calm down, but time seems to stand still. When it's finally over, you realize it has only been minutes.

When you can finally breathe again, you start to feel relief accompanied by a tinge of fear. What brought the panic attack on? When it will happen again? You may push these thoughts to the back of your mind and try to go about your day. However, you just can't shake off the baseline anxiety you now carry with you.

It always seems to lie just under the surface, and you feel like you can't even remember what it feels like to live without it.

Depression also seems to lie just under the surface. This mental disorder also weighs people down, but the root of this disorder is sadness—not fear. Again, we all experience sadness to some degree. However, those of us who struggle with depression face prolonged seasons of sadness that can be so intense we feel hopeless and even suicidal. It can be hard to get out of bed. We may feel like we have nothing to look forward to. We don't feel inspired at all. We feel like we are a burden to our loved ones. We are convinced that if they knew the horrifically dark thoughts that crossed our minds, they wouldn't want anything to do with us.

Married depressed people often think that their spouses are going to leave them. We often cry ourselves to sleep because the sadness won't subside. Sometimes, we aren't even sure why we are crying but the tears keep on coming. The body and mind of a depressed person are absolutely exhausted by the weight of the sadness, and we often feel like we are drowning with no hope of rescue.

It can be hard to simply get through a day doing our normal duties, and this can cause problems in our marriage, at our work, with our children, and with our friends. We feel guilty that we aren't the person we used to be. We feel like we are simply surviving rather than thriving. We feel lost and doomed to be depressed for the rest of our life, which terrifies us and only pulls us deeper into our depression. Christian people dealing with a depression often question their faith in the Lord. We ask ourselves questions like, "Did I not pray enough?" or "Am I really saved?" or "Do I just not have enough faith?" or "Did I do something to bring this on myself?" It's maddening.

Friend, can you relate? Are you suffering with anxiety and/or depression?

If so, I'm here to tell you that you are not alone. You did nothing to bring this on yourself. Most importantly, you can get the help you need. In fact, you must. I tell you this as someone who walked through a long battle with anxiety and depression.

I know how hard it is on a marriage and kids. I understand how it feels to wake up in the middle of the night in a cold sweat, having a full-blown anxiety attack, before running to the bathroom to throw up. I know the overwhelming fears of losing your spouse and the frustration of not being able to just "snap out of it." It's gut-wrenching and heart-breaking, but there is hope.

There is hope when we open up to our spouse and family about our struggle. We cannot keep it in. The only way we can get help is by being honest and open. Hope is not hiding in the dark; it can *only* be found in the light. So, we must be brave and bring our truth to light by sharing our deepest fears, worries, and anxieties with those we love most.

Personally, my anxiety and depression were most intense after I had my first child. What doctors initially diagnosed as postpartum depression turned into a four-year battle with clinical anxiety and depression. Those were some of the most difficult years of my life, and I don't know how I would have gotten through that time without the full support of my husband and the Lord's ever-present strength in my weakness.

There were times I would wake him up in the middle of the night—after hours of toiling with my anxiety and depression—to ask Dave for prayer and an encouraging word. No matter the hour and regardless of what he had to do in the morning, Dave lovingly prayed for me and encouraged me every single time. Even though I often had a hard time looking him in the eye because I was so ashamed of my struggle, he would gently raise my chin, look into my eyes, and tell me that he loved me and that God loved me.

He would remind me of who I am in Christ—a precious, priceless daughter of the King who can do all things through Christ who gives me strength. He would thank God in advance of the healing he was sure would come, and I would start to feel God's peace wash over me. I thank God that Dave encouraged me with God's truth in those extremely tender and vulnerable moments when my faith and hope were wavering.

I truly believe that God heard our prayers and strengthened both of us through that difficult time. Prayer has been and continues to be my lifeline of hope. Dave also encouraged me to go to regular Christian counseling. Attending counseling on a weekly basis was a tremendous help. Each session, my counselors would help me unpack the root of my depression and anxiety, give me practical tools to help with my healing, and remind of the truth of God's Word. I felt lighter and lighter with every appointment.

Today, I live in freedom, and I am quick to tell anyone suffering with depression and anxiety that you can live in freedom too! Your battle with anxiety and depression doesn't define your life. Every battle requires a fight, so we must keep fighting against anxiety and depression by resisting the desire to hide our struggles. Bring the negative thoughts in your mind to the light and surrender them to God. He will immerse you in His truth and show you that you are not damaged goods. Psalm 139:14 says that we are "fearfully and wonderfully made," and God doesn't want us to be anxious. Philippians 4:6-7 says,

Do not be anxious about anything, but in every situation, by prayer and petition, with thanksgiving, present your requests to God. And the peace of God, which transcends all understanding, will guard your hearts and your minds in Christ Jesus.

In John 14:27, Jesus tells us,

"Peace I leave with you; my peace I give you. I do not give to you as the world gives. Do not let your hearts be troubled and do not be afraid."

Friend, anxiety and depression are not easy enemies to face, and we certainly can't fight them alone. If you are struggling with either or both of these, please open up to your spouse, a trusted family member, or a close friend. Find a local Christian counselor or pastor to talk to on a regular basis. Inform your doctor, too. In certain situations, antidepressants or anti-anxiety medication may be helpful. Finding freedom from anxiety and/or depression often requires a multi-pronged approach.

You do not have to keep on suffering, and you *will* get through this. There will come a day when you *will* walk in freedom. It may take time–more time perhaps than you realize–but I promise that freedom will come when you refuse to give up and continue to get the help that you need. Let today be your first step to freedom.

Dave

When I was diagnosed with a thyroid disorder, I was prepared for physical setbacks but completely unprepared for the toll it would take on my mental health. Who knew that something located in your neck could have so much impact on your brain? As it turns out, thyroid disorders—and, in fact, many other physical disorders and diseases—can lead to rampant bouts of anxiety and depression.

It was interesting being on the other side of it after walking through those years with Ashley. When she struggled with intense anxiety and depression, I was honored to be a source of prayer and encouragement. But to be honest, I never thought I would struggle with anxiety and depression myself. I am not usually a "worrier." I tend to be optimistic. However, I've learned that anxiety and depression can plague *anyone*—regardless of things like personality, gender, age, upbringing, or socioeconomic situation.

As a quick point of clarification, I'm defining "depression" and "anxiety" in fairly broad terms. When I speak of *depression*, I'm referring to a prolonged sense of discouragement causing a person's default mood to be one of sadness. This causes a person to have a general numbness or negativity toward life. When I speak of *anxiety*, I'm referring to a prolonged struggle with nervousness or unnatural fear, which results in a lack of peace.

In our work with couples from all over the world, we've found that millions of couples suffer in silence over these mental health issues and the unnecessary stigmas they often carry. It's our goal to help these struggling couples find freedom and lasting solutions. We understand from experience the discouragement and isolation that results when depression or anxiety strikes, but remember: You're not alone. You will get through this.

I'm not a psychiatrist, so I'm not going to get too clinical here, but I do want to be very practical. In my own marriage and in my work with other marriages, I've seen depression and anxiety impact men differently than it impacts women. For example, depressed men are prone to respond in anger and frustration, but depressed women tend to feel more desperation and sadness. All are experiencing depression; it just manifests differently from person to person. Ashley has some excellent resources to help wives who are struggling with these same issues. She also wrote a powerful devotional that is helpful for both men and women. It's called *31 Verses and Prayers for the Anxious Mind and Heart,* and it's worth checking out if you or your spouse are struggling.

Before I share my own suggestions for those who are currently struggling with these issues, let me quickly recap of how anxiety and depression have impacted our marriage:

As Ashley shared earlier in this chapter, she endured a four-year battle with anxiety and depression that started with post-partum depression after the birth of our first son. Eventually it turned into a full-blown, clinical mental disorder. Through those early struggles, we learned to lean on each other, trust in God and relentlessly pursue healing. Ashley went to Christian counseling, read books, surrounded herself with encouraging influences, took a prescribed antidepressant, and prayed for healing. I did my part to reassure her during this struggle, and while I didn't always have the right words, I quickly learned that my steady presence meant more to her than my words ever could. I reassured her often of my love for her and my commitment to her. I always reminded her how God would carry us through this storm (which He did).

In more recent years, I've had my own struggle with various forms of anxiety and depression. My thyroid disorder was definitely a factor. Honestly, it's still a factor even as I write this. I'm generally a positive, upbeat guy, but I'm also prone to bouts of intense discouragement and melancholy. Walking through tragedies with close friends and relatives as I tried to minister to them has created seasons of great sadness. My driven, goal-oriented nature has set me up for a lot of discouragement over the years when life hasn't worked out as I hoped. That discouragement, left unchecked, can morph into seasons of depression.

My own medical issues have also created anxiety. My thyroid disorder has resulted in plummeting energy levels and testosterone levels. I've actively sought the right treatments and medications to restore those levels and I'm on the mend. But at my low points, I had very little sex drive and even sexual performance anxiety, stemming from low testosterone. For a guy in marriage ministry who specifically writes and speaks on sex, this often feels like a very intimate attack from Satan himself. Our enemy's MO is to "steal, kill, and destroy" (John 10:10), but our God is greater than any struggle the enemy throws our way.

Like a fingerprint, depression can look different for everybody. Despite its particular manifestations in each individual man or woman, there seem to be broad ways depression and anxiety transform men in general. Here are few warning signs to consider:

- You seem to have lost interest in things that once excited you.
- You are quick to react with anger and/or sadness, but slow to react with happiness or laughter.
- You often "zone out" and seem distant.
- You often escape into distractions such as the internet, television, etc.
- You become irrational, impatient, and easily irritable.
- You increase food and/or alcohol intake as a means of coping.
- You become fixated on negative thoughts.

If you're seeing any of these in your spouse or yourself, please get help! You can't "fix" the situation on your own, but you can take action that leads to healing. If you don't know where to start—whether to help yourself or your spouse—consider taking one or more of these steps:

- **Talk to a counselor.** A qualified counselor can guide you toward a positive breakthrough. I've personally experienced the positive impact of a great Christian counselor. Give counseling a try. It's a great first step.

· **Pray.** Prayer is powerful. God will use your prayers to change your situation, but He will also use your prayers to change your perspective. Ask for wisdom and strength. Then keep praying. God is with you in this. God loves you and will carry you through this. He will give you strength for the journey.

· **Refuel yourself.** When I've struggled with bouts of depression, I've had to be more intentional than ever about recharging my mind, body and soul. For me, this includes running and hiking outdoors, along with other forms of physical exercise. It also includes reading, prayer, listening to Christian music and other uplifting music, spending time with family and friends, and watching good comedy because laughter is good for the soul. Especially on the days when you don't feel like doing anything, force yourself to get out of bed and do something that recharges you.

· **Stay away from toxic forms of "comfort."** Depression leaves us vulnerable to unhealthy coping behaviors. These unhelpful outlets can include overeating, over-drinking, turning to counterfeit forms of intimacy (including pornography), and anything else that helps us numb ourselves against our environment rather than embracing a real and full life. If you've fallen into the trap of these unhealthy behaviors, don't beat yourself up. Shame is rarely helpful, but neither is wallowing in negative behaviors. Commit to healthy habits and seek accountability from a trusted friend or family member. Ask them to help make sure you're staying committed to healthier habits.

- **Stay connected to the people who love you.** There's a natural tendency to become a loner when you're feeling depressed, but you need relationships now more than ever. Don't push people away. Return texts and phone calls. In fact, be the one who initiates texts and phone calls. Gather with friends. Be present with your family. Prioritize your relationship with your spouse. Healing happens within relationships. Isolation tends to make problems worse.

- **Watch for warning signs in your spouse.** When your spouse is the one struggling, offer encouraging words but also be quick to promote action. Keep reassuring and encouraging them, but be on the lookout for moments that require tough love. You might need to say things like, *"I love you no matter what. I'm here for you no matter what, but I love you too much to allow you to keep living like this. God has a better plan for you and a better plan for us as a family. I'm not going anywhere, but I'm also not going to let you settle for this as the status quo. We are getting help. I'll be with you every step of the way, but you need to take action. Let's start with counseling. I'll go with you if you'd like."*

- **If you feel that you and/or your spouse might be at risk for suicide, don't wait to intervene.** Suicide has become a leading cause of death in our culture. To the irrational mind of a depressed person, suicide can seem like a way to end the suffering. They might even think everyone would be better off without them in their life. This is not the truth, and there is hope! If you feel your husband or wife might be at risk, please talk to a counselor or call one of the many suicide prevention hotlines to find solutions and steps to intervene.

I know that these moments can feel incredibly discouraging and isolating, but you will get through this. From experience, I can tell you that we serve a God who will never leave you or forsake you. I pray that Christ, "The Prince of Peace," would bring peace to your hearts and your homes as you trust Him in these moments of great struggle.

Ashley

As I stated earlier, millions suffer from the debilitating effects of anxiety and depression every day, and these struggles can be especially hard on a marriage. Depression and anxiety are genuine mental health issues, but the symptoms can easily go unnoticed and are therefore misunderstood. It's difficult for a spouse who isn't depressed and anxious to fully understand what their husband or wife is going through, or why they are having such a difficult time with the pressures of daily life. This lack of understanding—and sometimes a lack of patience—only makes the depression and anxiety worse. It can damage the marriage.

So, how can a spouse support his or her anxious and/or depressed spouse? First of all, do your best to understand what your partner is going through. If you are a non-depressive, non-anxiety-prone person, you probably deal with worry very differently from your spouse.

We often say that a strong marriage rarely has two strong people at the same time. Therefore, you must take turns being strong for each other. If your spouse is going through anxiety and/or depression, they desperately need you to be strong for them. Being "strong" doesn't mean having all the answers. It simply means your love and presence provide a steady source of consistency from which your spouse can draw strength during the moments when they feel weak.

Before I share solutions for those struggling with these issues, I think it is important to help those who have never experienced anxiety or depression to better understand the daily experience of your depressed/anxious spouse. Imagine that you are jumping off a diving board into a swimming pool. As you plunge into the water, you start to sink down but quickly move your arms to make your way up to the surface to breathe. This is normal behavior. This is how we are supposed to deal with worry. The worry may enter our minds, but we quickly find a way to propel ourselves out of it...whether through talking about it, thinking about it, reading Scripture, praying, etc. When we handle worry appropriately, we don't remain in that state of worry. We pass through it. We come back to the surface.

Now, imagine that you jump off the diving board, hit the water, and begin to sink lower and lower. Your arms don't move. Your chest starts to burn from the lack of oxygen. You feel the enormous weight of the water all around you. You try to swim upward, but you can't find your way up to the surface. You are stuck, paralyzed by fear. You know you'll find comfort and safety at the surface, but the weight is just too heavy.

This is precisely how it feels when your spouse experiences an anxiety attack or ongoing anxiety and depression. These are more than just worrisome thoughts. They may want to "shake it off," but the process is much more complicated than that.

Here are five things your depressed/anxious spouse desperately wants you to know:

1.   Their anxiety can be emotionally paralyzing and physically limiting at times.

I believe that this is the hardest reality for those without anxiety and depression to understand. When your spouse experiences anxious moments, their thoughts become stuck on the worry or stress they are enduring. It's like a bird found a way to build a nest in your spouse's head. Then the bird laid eggs. Then the eggs hatch and the new birds start laying their own eggs. Anxiety has a way of multiplying exponentially, and when this happens it can manifest itself into a full-blown anxiety attack. Your spouse's heart starts racing, they begin to sweat, they may experience stomach pains, nausea, vomiting, diarrhea, trouble breathing, and even heart palpitations. Though anxiety attacks eventually pass, they can paralyze him or her for that moment, and are as real as any sickness.

2.   They are not crazy.

As I described earlier, an anxious mind works differently than a non-anxious mind, but that doesn't mean that your husband or wife is "crazy." In fact, an anxious or depressed person can be hard to identify because he or she often puts on a happy face. They can be high-functioning. Your spouse probably tries to hide their episodes of anxiety and depression because they don't want to burden you or the family. Your spouse is all too aware of their anxiety and depression...and that causes them to spiral further into those issues. This difficulty coping emotionally or mentally can last for a short season or many seasons.

3.   They can often recognize anxiety and/or depression for what it is.

Most of the time, a person knows they are not thinking clearly when struggling with anxiety or depression. Your spouse most likely realizes that they are anxious and/or depressed. They sincerely desire to get better, but don't know where to start. They may feel like a sailboat just waiting for the wind to catch the sail. They need the wind and know it can blow them into safer, calmer waters. But the wind never seems to blow their way. This makes them more anxious and depressed.

4. They need your patience, support, and compassion.

Overcoming anxiety is a process that takes plenty of prayer, time, and counseling. Sometimes, our brains need medication to regain and maintain the proper levels of serotonin. I went through years of counseling before I felt like I was able to overcome my anxiety.

Dave played an instrumental role in my recovery. He never told me to "snap out of it." He would listen to me talk about my feelings for hours on end. He prayed with me constantly and would remind me of the truth of God's Word. He helped me find a good counselor and showed me great compassion during the many nights I would cry myself to sleep.

I often felt guilty that I couldn't shake the anxiety, and I remember telling Dave that he deserved a better wife who wasn't crazy. He would always take my hands, stare straight into my eyes, and assure me that I was his one and only. He told me we would get through this together. I don't think I would have recovered without his steadfast support, patience, and compassion. I am forever thankful to him for truly living out the marital vow of "in sickness and in health" during those long, difficult years.

5. There is hope in recovery!

I have experienced firsthand the tremendous hope that arrives in recovery from anxiety and depression, and my supportive, encouraging, and prayerful husband played a huge part in this. You can be a massive help to your spouse as well! More than anything, your partner needs to know that you won't give up on them. Your spouse needs to know you believe they will get better. Please don't add to their anxiety by trying to rush the recovery process or doubting that they will ever be able to recover in the first place.

During this process, please choose your words carefully. Encourage them to get help. Take them to the doctor, psychologist or counselor. Just don't give up on your spouse or decide that they will never be able to enjoy a life without constant anxiety or depression. That is just not true. Remember these scriptures:

"Do not be anxious about anything, but in every situation, by prayer and petition, with thanksgiving, present your requests to God." (Philippians 4:6)

"For God has not given us the spirit of fear, but of power, and love, and self-control." (2 Timothy 1:7 MEV)

"No, in all these things we are more than conquerors through him who loved us." (Romans 8:37)

God clearly doesn't want any of us to live with anxious or depressed minds. It is my prayer that you and your spouse will work together to find freedom from anxiety and peace in your home. He *will* get you both through this!

CHAPTER 3:

Listening to the Right Voices

Ashley

A few years ago, at the XO Marriage Conference, I told a true story about how the right voices can change your life for the better, but the wrong voices can throw us off course. We have to learn to listen to the right voices. This principle holds true in all parts of life. When you choose to give healthy advice and surround yourself with people who will speak healthy advice to you, every aspect of your life can benefit.

I'd like to share that same story with you now. I remember the conversation vividly. My friends and I were driving to the beach for a girls' trip, and I rode with one of those ladies in her minivan. We shared funny stories and laughed until our stomachs hurt for the first hour-and-a-half, but then she turned sullen for the final 30 minutes of the drive. The van became quiet. With tears in her eyes and a shaky voice, my friend told me she was going to leave her husband because she didn't love him anymore. As I listened to her reasoning, I silently prayed that God would give me the words to help my hurting friend give her marriage another chance. Here's what I shared with her...

Every marriage has seasons of disappointment, frustration, and grind. Sometimes we bring it on ourselves with bad choices or careless mistakes. Other times, we're blindsided by an unforeseen catastrophe. It's easy to point fingers during those times. It's easy to shut down, stop talking, and internalize bitterness or shame. However, those heavy, vulnerable moments—when our hearts are broken, and we leave thousands of words unspoken—are the very moments that we need to lean into our spouse the most.

This world tells us that love is a feeling that can come and go. If this is true, then love will fail us every time. It will never be enough to hold a marriage together. This is *not* at all how God defines love. The Bible tells us in 1 Corinthians 13 that true love is unconditional. It doesn't keep a record of wrongs. It protects us. It heals us. True love never fails us!

Even so, there may be moments when we feel like giving up on our spouse and ending our marriage. Why is this? It's because we don't foresee the healing in our future. We don't want to put in the work and take the time to get to the root issues.

We'd rather just start over, but what we fail to see is that marriage is a lasting commitment we will always carry with us, regardless of whether or not we move on. God designed it this way. It's not something we can just shake off and forget.

When we marry, we pledge to give every part of ourselves to our spouse. And we trust them to do the same. Our world tends to frown on this today because it means we have to be completely vulnerable, putting our hearts on the line. This is the beautiful mystery of marriage. When both partners do this to the best of their abilities—consciously choosing to bear their naked souls before one another, holding nothing back—there is an incredible, intimate union that forms. The more we pursue God and one another, the tighter the bond becomes.

Most of us go into our marriages wanting this amazing union with our partner. However, life gets in the way, and we forget to be intentional with our time. Our marriage gets put on the back burner as a result, but this is counter to what God wants for our marriage and family.

Our spouse deserves our time and attention every single day whether or not they have earned it. We give these things to our spouse because we love them, and we're devoted to making our marriage thrive.

There will be seasons when we don't feel like giving our spouse time and attention. There will be moments when...

we feel like we're just roommates.
we feel like he/she isn't giving us what we want.
we don't feel attracted to our spouse anymore.
the thought of talking with them is exhausting.
it feels like we can't do anything right.
we wonder if the marriage was a mistake.
we decide to stay together "just for the kids."
we aren't sure if we can trust a spouse anymore.
we've fallen out of love with our spouse.
we have a secret that we're not sure we can ever share with our spouse.
we hate being married, but don't know what to do about it.

These situations can be hurtful, confusing, and potentially devastating to a marriage, but they are not a reason to give up. We must be willing and determined to fight for our marriage. Certainly, it takes both the husband and wife to make it work, but we must be willing to be the one to take the first step. Do those things you enjoyed doing together when you were dating.

Visit that place you've always wanted to go together. Go see a Christian marriage counselor to learn how to have a healthier relationship. Attend a couple's retreat to strengthen your marriage. Surround yourself with couples whose marriages are strong. Pray together and ask God to soften your hearts towards one another. Be intentional about increasing your physical affection and make love often. Don't hold back. Share what's on your heart. Be honest and open. Don't keep secrets of any kind from one another.

Remember: As husband and wife, you have vowed to be each other's partner, lover, best friend, encourager, accountability, and the person they lean on when hurting or weak. Marriage is a beautiful, lifelong partnership when we allow it to be. However, we can't give up when it gets hard. We *must* do our best to press on.

That weekend trip was a turning point for the friend I referenced earlier. Once we arrived at the beach, she shared her decision to divorce her husband with another friend, and that friend also encouraged her to keep fighting for her marriage. The three of us ended up praying together during that trip. Although we did a lot of listening—as we should all do when a friend has something heavy on their heart—my friends and I were also able to speak into her situation.

Dave and I certainly don't have a perfect marriage, nor do we have all the answers. But we know Who does. God doesn't abandon us when we have marital problems. He was right there for my friend when she needed Him most, and He is there for you, too. My friend and her husband decided to fight for their marriage with God's help. That was almost a decade ago. They did the hard work, and they fully surrendered their relationship to the Lord. Today, their marriage is better than ever. I love seeing the smiles on their faces and the great love and respect they have for one another. I feel like I've witnessed a marriage miracle, and my friend remains so thankful that she refused to give up on her husband.

Dave

There's such power in listening to the right voices, but sometimes the right—or wrong—voice can sound exactly like what you're telling yourself. Negative self-talk keeps so many people stuck in an unhealthy rut. We can't allow reinforced negative thinking to play on repeat in our minds. Let me share an embarrassing story from my past to illustrate this point.

When I was in the eighth grade (long before I met my true love, Ashley), I had a crush on a girl in my class named Angie. I was a pretty dorky kid in middle school, but despite my adolescent awkwardness, I managed to summon the courage to start conversations with her whenever I could. My so-called courage was actually just a combination of raging hormones and unrealistic optimism, but it felt extremely brave to my eighth-grade brain. That was good enough for me.

My voice would crack, and my palms would get sweaty, but with each conversation she would smile politely while dodging the spit particles that flew off my braces as I spoke. I interpreted her smile to mean that she was interested in me. We'd never actually had a conversation that lasted more than thirty seconds, but I was pretty sure she wanted to spend more time with me, to the degree I wanted to spend more time with her.

I was convinced that when she looked at me, she didn't see my braces and acne. She saw Prince Charming.

Our teenage romance was off to a stellar start until the fateful day when everything unraveled in one of the most terrifying moments of my life. We were standing in science class, where I had cornered her for a chat, when I suddenly felt a draft of air on my legs.

I heard laughter behind me, and Angie's face turned a bright shade of red. She covered her face and giggled and quickly ran off, leaving me trying to figure out what had just happened. I looked down slowly, and to my horror, my sweatpants were down at my ankles.

(Yes, I wore sweatpants to school. Don't judge me! In the early nineties in central Kentucky, they were still a socially acceptable middle school wardrobe option. That was, however, the last day I ever wore sweatpants anywhere, because you just can't trust the drawstring on those things.)

This particular wardrobe malfunction was not the result of a faulty drawstring. It was an act of sabotage. My so-called "friend" Nick had grabbed my pants from behind and yanked them to the floor. God had mercy on me that day and somehow kept my Fruit of the Loom underwear from making the trip downward with my pants. Had my "tighty whiteys" also gone to the floor, I'd still be in counseling.

I pulled my pants back up to my waist with ninja-like reflexes, but the damage had been done. I was humiliated. Nick had put me in the most vulnerable and exposed position possible. But instead of receiving compassion and encouragement from a girl I really liked, I felt the sting of rejection. We never really talked after that. It was probably more because of my own embarrassment than anything else.

I share this funny story not because it's an example of true rejection, but because it illustrates vulnerability in relationships and how our past experiences can shape our views of love. Love requires vulnerability, and when that exposure results in rejection, our defense mechanisms can actually work against us. They may even sabotage our current relationships. With military precision, we safeguard certain parts of ourselves in order to prevent the humiliation or rejection we have felt in the past.

I wore a tightly cinched belt for years after that sweatpants incident.

Of course, we've all faced relational challenges far more significant than an embarrassing middle school prank. When we've been rejected, abandoned, or abused by the very people who should have been protecting us, the ramifications can be deep and long lasting. If you've experienced the sting of betrayal by a close friend, parent, sibling, or even spouse, you know exactly the pain I'm talking about. The more you love someone, the more potential that person has to hurt you.

But until you become truly vulnerable—giving a person the ability to hurt you—you'll never truly be able to experience love. This reality keeps some people from committing to a relationship with their whole hearts because they're trying to protect themselves from being wounded again. But if we're not careful, our wounds from the past can create new wounds in the present. It is a Catch-22 that can keep our relationships in perpetual dysfunction until we become intentional about seeking healing from the past and moving forward in a healthy way.

Ashley

We must always seek out the ultimate voice of truth—the Lord and His Word— to make sure we're staying on the right path. One of the core values in the Willis household is honesty. Our kids know that they can get in trouble for lots of things, but lying tops the list. We put so much value on honesty because we want our kids to realize that love is built on trust. So, if we want to keep our family strong, we've got to always tell each other the truth.

We went through several years when the kids learned this tell-the-truth lesson so well that it nearly backfired on us. They assumed that because the truth was so important, if they considered something to be true, they should say it out loud. On the surface, this doesn't seem like a bad thing—until we had some very embarrassing interactions in public.

Here are a few examples from the long list of unfiltered "truths" that my children spoke to strangers in public:

> *"Wow, you have a huge belly!"*
> *"You look really old like Yoda."*
> *"You smell funny."*
> *"Why are you dressed like that? Are you homeless?"*
> *"Are you going to feed milk to the baby from your nipples?"*

Yeah! That last one was actually addressed to Dave, who was holding a baby at the time. He then held the baby up close to his hairy nipple as if about to breastfeed, which was both disgusting and hilarious. The kids cackled with delight.

As you can imagine, we preferred those kinds of phrases to not be blurted out in public to complete strangers. A lot of these incidents seemed to happen at Walmart. I love Walmart, but we could have saved some trouble by not taking our kids there.

We knew that isolating the kids at home until adulthood wouldn't work, so we needed a new strategy that kept the emphasis on truth but also added a filter to the process. Our friends, the Asselin family, had a policy that worked great, so we decided to make it part of our family standards as well.

They taught their kids that they weren't allowed to say anything to anyone unless it met three criteria:

1. It had to be *true.*
2. It had to be *kind.*
3. It had to be *necessary.*

TKN: True, Kind, and Necessary.

This became our mantra as well. We taught our kids that truth is vital, but the truth alone isn't enough. You can say something that is technically right, but if you say it without love and compassion, you are still wrong. We quickly encountered a real-world testing ground to try the new policy.

Yes, it was at Walmart. Our older two boys were around ages 3 and 5. The boys were hovering around the cart looking for candy to sneak in while I wasn't looking. An elderly woman, who looked to be around ninety years old, slowly walked by. The boys couldn't help but stare. I don't think they had ever seen someone that old before. I held my breath as the boys started to say something. They quickly caught themselves and bit their tongues.

Then, while she was still just a few steps away, they shouted with pride, "Mom! Mom! We did it! That really old lady just walked by, and we didn't even tell her that she looked old like Yoda from *Star Wars*!"

I patted the boys on the head while giving an awkward smile to the sweet lady, simultaneously praying she didn't hear one word of their commentary. Like most life lessons, this was a work in progress. I'm happy to report that the boys have gotten much better at it through the years, thank the Lord.

Speaking the truth in love doesn't mean you should never communicate a painful truth to someone. In fact, the Bible teaches that painful truths from a friend can be trusted, but an enemy just tells you what you want to hear (Proverbs 27:6). A mark of true friendship and real love is a commitment to be the one to speak a painful truth. Sometimes this will involve little things, like when a friend or relative is willing to tell you there's spit-up on your blouse, toothpaste in your hair, or something stuck in your teeth.

A mere acquaintance or enemy would just walk away, giggling and leaving you to figure it out on your own.

However, this principle also holds true in bigger issues. If you're in an unhealthy relationship with someone of the opposite sex who isn't your spouse, or if you've developed some dangerous or self-destructive habits, a loved one will have the courage to intervene. They'll refuse to just tell you what you want to hear. Even if you hate them for saying it, they'll say it anyway, because they love you and truly care about you and your family.

Dave

I learned a valuable lesson about life when I decided to coach my son Cooper's basketball team when he was five years old. I knew almost nothing about basketball. I played pickup games in my school days, but my lack of height and nonexistent vertical leaping ability—not to mention my prominent love handles—made me a less-than-ideal draft pick for the sport.

In addition to my very limited knowledge, I also had no expertise in herding five-year-olds. You've got to have a lot of love and a ridiculous amount of patience to teach kids at that age. (When you kindergarten teachers get to heaven, you'll definitely be the ones living in the gated community.)

I was fearful about coaching, but my apprehension was outweighed by my love for my son. Love is powerful, so when you put your love against your fear, love will win every time. Cooper wanted me to coach, and I looked into those puppy dog eyes and said, "Sure, buddy! I'd love to coach your team!"

I had high hopes of turning those energetic whippersnappers into future Olympians. I quickly learned that we needed to start with the basics: dribbling the ball instead of running with it, not hugging other players during the game, not hugging the referees during the game, and keeping the ball inbounds. Surprisingly, of all the lessons I attempted to teach them, the concept of keeping the ball inbounds proved to be the toughest lesson for them to grasp.

At first, the white outlines around the court were meaningless to the kids. Once they started bouncing the ball, they just kept going with no regard for the boundaries. They also didn't seem to be able to hear me blowing the whistle and shouting for them to stop. They would often end up outside the gym before I could get to them. Five-year-olds are much faster than they look.

Midway through the season, though, the concept of boundaries finally clicked. That's when the real game actually started. Until they learned to keep the ball inbounds, it didn't matter how fast they ran or how hard they played. If it wasn't inbounds, it didn't count.

If you want to make sure you're listening to the right voices, you need to be clear about what's "out-of-bounds" in your life. If you don't set your own standards, other people will set standards for you. God gave us the Bible to be a roadmap for life and to provide clear boundaries that help us determine what's true and what's a dangerous lie.

Make the decision to keep your life inbounds. Refuse to be influenced by voices who would tempt you to step out-of-bounds and compromise on God's standards or your own integrity. Do it for the integrity of your marriage and family. The lesson of staying inbounds isn't just for kindergarten basketball players. It's a lesson we all need through every season of life.

Ashley

I love those memories of Dave coaching our boys. He was always quick to encourage the kids on the team, but he was also willing to share difficult truths to help the kids get better. Part of being a good coach (or a good spouse or a good friend) requires sharing difficult truths with love. We all need people in our lives who love us enough to help us see our own blind spots—and we *all* have blind spots.

I remember a time when I was really struggling with losing weight and cultivating a consistent, doable exercise routine. I was sharing my frustrations with my longtime friend, Michelle, during the dinner portion of one of our small group meetings. Michelle and I, along with our families, had been in the same small group for seven years, so we knew the details of each other's lives very well. Michelle had seen me yo-yo dieting, week after week, as I tried out the latest diet craze of the day—always to no avail. One week, we planned a huge spaghetti dinner. Each family brought something delicious. But instead of simply taking a small portion for myself, I didn't eat anything at all because it didn't "fit" with the latest diet I had adopted that week.

When Michelle asked why I wasn't eating anything and I told her why, she just smiled at me with compassion. Then, she asked me if I had been running lately. I said no and began to explain that I'm "just not a runner." I listed off other excuses. In that moment, Michelle decided to lovingly press me a little.

She smiled again and said, "Ashley, you know that you really can do anything you put your mind to. I've seen you do it many times. You just have to decide and then stick with it. When you do, you won't have to be so restrictive with your diet, and you can enjoy food again. I'd be happy to run with you sometimes. It would be fun!"

I listened with another excuse on the tip of my tongue, but the Holy Spirit used Michelle's wise words to convict me in that moment. It wasn't a slap-in-the-face conviction. It was much more like a gentle nudge, encouraging me to stop the madness of extreme diets and fitness crazes only to end up failing at them, then going back to doing nothing for my health. Michelle's truthful, kind, and necessary words were exactly what I needed to hear.

That was a pivotal moment for me in my health journey. I am so grateful that she didn't simply tell me what she thought I wanted to hear in that moment. She helped me get out of the cycle of self-sabotage. As a friend who truly cared about me, she lovingly told me the hard truth because she knew it could be very helpful to me—even if it initially stung my pride.

Think back over your life. Have there ever been times you've had someone express a deep and sincere concern for you by pointing out a painful truth? That's the mark of a real friend. The truth isn't always comfortable, but it's always necessary. Sometimes speaking a difficult truth is something you'll have to do for yourself. We must always remain open to the Holy Spirit's conviction and embrace repentance instead of making excuses for our actions. We all tend to craft a self-focused view of the world in which we emerge as either a hero or a victim in every scene. We're never the villains in the story.

However, the truth is that we've all been the villain more often than we'd like to admit. A life of love requires that we look in the mirror and give an honest and humble self-assessment.

Jesus once pointed out that we human beings seem to be experts at noticing a speck of sawdust in somebody else's eye, while ignoring the wooden plank sticking out of our own eye. We can be so quick to see the flaws in others and so blind to the obvious flaws in ourselves. We tend to create a hierarchy of sin in which our sins aren't nearly as bad as somebody else's. We become experts at pointing our fingers at people who are "worse" than we are, which makes us feel justified in our sin.

For instance, imagine you fudge the numbers on your taxes. You think, "It's no big deal! The government doesn't need that money. They'd just blow it. I worked hard for this. Maybe it's technically wrong, but there are worse things I could be doing on my computer than creative accounting on my taxes. The guy who shares my cubicle at work looks at porn on his computer! That's way worse, right?"

And the guy who looks at pornography might say, "So what? I look at porn. I'm a grown man, and I can do what I want. It's not hurting anybody. It's just fantasy. At least I'm not like my boss. She's actually cheating on her husband. What I'm doing isn't as bad as an actual affair, right?"

And the boss might say, "So, I'm having an affair. I'm not proud of it, but I am a woman with needs. It's not even against the law. I could be doing much worse things. Like the guy we fired for stealing. He got arrested. He's in prison for embezzlement. That's worse than what I'm doing, right?"

And the embezzler might say, "So I stole some money, but I never hurt anybody. My cell mate has killed a guy! That's way worse than what I did, right?"

And the cellmate might say, "Okay, you got me. I killed a guy, but it was only one guy and he wasn't even nice! I'm nothing like the guy on death row down the hall. He's a serial killer! He's killed lots of people! That's way worse than on murder, right?"

And the serial killer might respond, "So I'm a serial killer. Nobody's perfect. But don't be too quick to judge me, because I never once cheated on my taxes!"

You get the idea! We are always ready and willing to puff ourselves up and point the finger at somebody else. Until we can look in the mirror and come to terms with our own sin and desperate need for God's grace, we'll never be able to see ourselves or others through the lens of love. God wants us to have a heart for loving unlovable people, because that's what He did for us! He loved us much more than we could ever deserve, and He calls us to do the same for others. Our own mental health requires seeing *ourselves* through God's eyes while also seeing *others* through His eyes.

In the next chapter, we'll transition from exploring mental health issues to looking at ways to improve physical health. Our mental health and physical health are more closely connected than you may realize. A healthy mind can help create a healthier body and vice versa. Physical health isn't just about superficial goals or personal appearance. It's also about honoring yourself, honoring your spouse and honoring the God who created your body to be the temple where He dwells. He wants us to glorify Him with our bodies and enjoy our physical health to the fullest. Wherever you currently are in your physical health journey, I believe the next section will encourage you.

SECTION TWO:

BODY

*Don't you realize that your body is the
temple of the Holy Spirit, who lives
in you and was given to you by God?
You do not belong to yourself, for God
bought you with a high price. So, you
must honor God with your body.*

1 Corinthians 6:19-20 (NLT)

CHAPTER 4:

In Thickness and in Health

Ashley

Dave and I were recently going through a box of old photos, and we found one that made us laugh until our stomachs hurt. Laughter has been the only consistent abdominal workout we've enjoyed together. It's way more fun than planks and crunches, which is why we watch reruns of *The Office* much more often than we do sit-ups. The photos that made us cackle were "before pictures" we took before starting a new fitness plan around 15 years ago. The plan was based on the popular book *Body for Life*. It was a 90-day fitness strategy that included a very structured diet plan and exercise regimen.

This program was trending at the time, and like I shared in the last chapter, we used to jump on the bandwagon of every new fitness craze: Billy Blanks' Tae Bo DVDs, the Atkins Diet, Beach Body, Jenny Craig, Weight Watchers, and a multitude of other plans now gathering dust in our garage. The program challenged all participants to take a "before" picture and then an "after" picture once the 90-day challenge was complete. We were so determined to make *Body for Life* work that we obeyed this instruction.

We stripped down to our swimsuits, intending to capture the last "chubby picture" we'd ever take. We both pushed our guts out over our belt lines—this was easy since we both were out of shape and had minor love handles already—and we smiled for the photo.

Unfortunately, we never actually made it to the "after" photo. We failed miserably on the plan. In fact, we actually gained a little weight over those couple of weeks. Ironically, we ended up being in better shape for the "before" photo than we were a few weeks later. Go figure! It wasn't the plan's fault. It was our own fault for not actually *following* the plan.

Part of the reason for our failure was that the *Body for Life* program had a built-in "free day" when you could eat whatever you wanted. Calories didn't count. This free day was our idea of heaven! We started the program on the free day by feasting on a gluttonous fat fest of junk food. Each of us probably packed away thousands of calories in that single day. We overdid it so much that we woke up the next morning with what felt like a food hangover. We didn't have the energy or motivation to actually start the plan.

We limped through the next few days, telling ourselves we'd start the program strong the following week. We pinpointed Day One of *Body for Life*. And then 24 hours before *that* day, we decided we should have one last free day and...repeated the whole process from the week before.

If nothing else, we were really committed to the idea of free days.

This process actually happened for several more weeks. We never got around to dedicating more than a couple days at a time to the actual plan. We went all-in on the free day concept, but fizzled out when it came to the actual health part.

We laugh about it now, but our trend-chasing, quick-fix, yo-yo dieting strategies back then just weren't a sustainable path to lasting health. Over the last twenty years, we've learned a lot and settled into a much more manageable rhythm—with much healthier habits. We're certainly not fitness models, but we are in better shape than we were fifteen years ago, when we were in our mid-twenties. We are appreciating this current season of life and marriage because we learned the hard way that neglecting our health ends up costing us in the long run.

On our wedding day, we took the vow "In sickness and in health." Later we joked that we should have said, "In *thickness* and in health." Over two-plus decades together, we've both experienced fairly drastic highs and lows in our weights, our energy levels, our sex drives, and nearly every other aspect of overall health. In some seasons, we've cheered each other on as great accountability partners on our journey toward betterhealth. In other seasons, we've enabled each other to overindulge and perpetuate an unhealthy lifestyle.

We've suffered setbacks, too, including weight gain, physical issues (Dave's thyroid disorder), mental health setbacks (my anxiety and depression), and the hormonal imbalances that have affected us both. On the positive side, we've enjoyed numerous health victories along the way. We've hit target-weight goals, completed distance races, and maintained a long streak of daily, multimile walks together. Even as we write this book, we are training to complete our longtime shared goal of hiking Peru's Inca Trail to Machu Picchu together.

We're not claiming to be fitness gurus, but we have personally experienced the benefits of prioritizing physical health. We tend to be at our best for one another when we're both feeling healthy and energetic. The marriage becomes healthier as a result. When we go through prolonged seasons of apathy related to physical health, we end up paying a high price individually and also within our marriage.

Dave

Part of why Ashley and I failed at *Body for Life* is because we committed one of our culture's most common mistakes: we were impatient. We wanted the "after" picture to appear instantaneously without having to suffer through the work. In all parts of life, health and marriage, disciplined work is important. I've looked for shortcuts, but there aren't any worth taking.

In 1972, Stanford University conducted a groundbreaking study that unearthed a powerful insight into human behavior and relationships. The test was simple, but the results proved to be profound. Hundreds of children from all walks of life were brought onto campus and given what is now famously known as "The Marshmallow Test." The instructions were very basic. Each child was asked to sit down at a table. A researcher would place a marshmallow in front of the hungry kid and then delivered this proposition: "You can eat this marshmallow right now. Or, if you don't eat it now and wait until I get back, I'll give you two marshmallows to eat."

Each participant could have one now or two later. That was the test. Many kids would gobble up the marshmallow even before they heard the rules. Others would wait a little while, but eventually their willpower would disappear, and they'd give in and eat it. A few kids actually found the inner strength to wait. They refused to settle for one marshmallow when patience would double the prize.

The kids who resisted the temptation didn't usually do it by willpower alone. They wouldn't just sit still and stare at the marshmallow. They got up and played and pretended the marshmallow wasn't even there until the researcher came back and gave them two. They beat temptation by removing the single marshmallow as an option, because they resolved that a better option was coming. It was well worth the wait.

This study was so valuable because the researchers followed those kids into adulthood and continued to measure their progress in different areas of their lives. They recorded profound differences between the "one-marshmallow kids" and the "two-marshmallow kids." The kids who had shown restraint—who waited for two marshmallows—were statistically much more likely to have a successful career, financial stability, and a long-term marriage.

In short, the study determined that the one factor most likely to determine an individual's lifelong health and happiness wasn't ethnicity, gender, family of origin, or even intelligence. The most important factor in determining the long-term health and vitality of a person's life and relationships was connected to a single discipline: the ability to delay gratification. In other words, patience is one of the most critical life skills a person can possess.

Intuitively, we know this to be true, and yet it can be so difficult to put into practice. I know that patience is important, but I've struggled with it all my life. I'd like to think I would have been a "two-marshmallow kid," but I doubt I would have been. I catch myself watching the lines at Walmart and estimating which one will go fastest. If I end up choosing a slow line, I nearly have a panic attack. Then, if the person in line ahead of me pays with a check—which takes forever—and tries to balance their checkbook while I'm waiting, I have to restrain myself from shouting, "Who pays with a check? What decade do you live in?"

I clearly have some ongoing struggles related to patience. It's a life lesson I'm still trying to learn.

(My apologies if you still pay with checks. I don't judge you, although I do encourage you to consider the life-changing technology of a debit card. If nothing else, they'll make your Walmart checkout much faster!)

Ashley

Love is patient (1 Corinthians 13:1), but we still live in a very impatient world. We watch our shows "on demand." We use DVRs to fast-forward through commercials. We use express lanes at the grocery store, and when someone gets in front of us with too many items in their cart, we act like a felony has been committed. We hate traffic, long lines, waiting rooms, and anything or anyone who interrupts our agenda. In general, we're impatient, and we want everything right now! We live in a "one marshmallow now" kind of society.

This on-demand mentality has also swarmed into our relationships. It threatens to replace the patience of love with the immediacy of pleasure. We're tempted to make compromises so we can extract the positive feelings of love without the time and commitment love requires. In our impatience and selfishness, our culture has attempted to redefine love and embraced damaging compromises in the process.

We've traded porn for true intimacy. We've traded committed marriages for commitment-free cohabitation. We've traded meaningful conversations for text messages. We've traded "'til death do us part" for divorce. We've traded the pursuit of holiness for the pursuit of happiness. We've traded love for lust. We've attempted to exploit all the benefits and pleasures of love without investing the commitment and self-sacrifice that love requires.

We may say we value love, but too often our actions prove we value other things much more. So many of us, including myself, struggle with many of these temptations. I've been impatient too many times in my life, but I truly want to be a "two marshmallows later" kind of woman. I know I can't do this on my own, but I also know that I can have more patience with God's help. In fact, patience is a literal "fruit of the spirit" (Galatians 5:22). In other words, it is one of the gifts that God gives us when we choose to follow Him.

He knows that patience will bless our life and relationships. That is precisely why it is a gift that He gives us when we enter into a relationship with Him. He helps us to delay gratification. He helps us stay strong in moments when we feel tempted to stray from the right path. He knows that we all desperately need patience in our lives, and He is quick to give it to us when we seek Him.

The Lord has helped me tremendously in this area of developing more patience and discipline in my life. If you struggle with this, I know He can help you, too! Everything worth having is worth waiting for and working for, especially when it comes to our health.

Dave

The good news is that we don't have to achieve health all at once. It happens incrementally with consistent, small steps in the right direction. When I was in college, I worked the night shift for two summers at a Toyota plant in Georgetown, Kentucky. I didn't enjoy the vampire schedule of sleeping during the day and staying up all night, but I was making more than double the minimum wage. For a college kid, I felt like I'd hit the jackpot! While my friends were eating ramen noodles, I was feasting like a king on pizza and Taco Bell. Life was good.

As valuable as that paycheck was to me, the most valuable asset I took away from that experience wasn't the money. It was a single word within the Toyota company culture—and the philosophy behind that word. This word would have a transformative impact on my future marriage, career, and every other important aspect of my life. It was the Japanese word *kaizen,* which has guided Toyota and countless companies around the world. *Kaizen* simply means "to improve continuously."

At Toyota, I was introduced to a culture where, even though profits were already high and the operation was already running smoothly, nobody was content to rest on past successes. There was a constant and continuous movement toward improvement, which impacted every aspect of the company and every individual within it. Finding ways to shave even a fraction of a second off the assembly line process could mean the difference of millions of dollars over a period of a few years. Every improvement, big or small, was implemented and celebrated.

Kaizen applies to more than just building better cars. It can also be leveraged to build better relationships. I want you to imagine how your life would look if, each day, you found a way to make your relationships a little better than they were the day before. Now imagine how every aspect of your life could improve in the process. It's possible—and it's completely within your power to make it a reality. Even the tiniest of positive changes, implemented consistently over time, have the power to produce a completely new reality for your marriage.

Ashley

Part of what holds us back from embracing a physically healthy lifestyle is that we buy into myths that tell us we're just not cut out to be in shape. The truth is, you are a warrior! You need to believe what God says about you and not the false, negative voices trying to talk you out of your full potential.

Whenever we find ourselves in a place where feelings are incompatible with God's truth, we've got to trust God over our feelings. This is especially important when it comes to understanding our own identity. We can't look within ourselves to discover who we are; we can only look to the one who created us.

In the sixth chapter of the Book of Judges, the Bible tells us the story of a man who struggled with his identity. His name was Gideon. He lived in a time of chaos and uncertainty. Israel had been invaded by an army of brutal oppressors, and the people of Israel lived in terror.

When we're introduced to Gideon, he's hiding in a cave, threshing wheat in a winepress. He's doing whatever he can to stay alive, but it's clear that he's terrified and confused. God sends an angel to remind Gideon who he is. Isn't that amazing? The angel shows up and greets Gideon by saying, "Mighty hero, the LORD is with you!" (Judges 6:12).

Gideon was probably left scratching his head, thinking the angel must have been talking to somebody else. Gideon didn't *look* like a mighty hero. Honestly, the Bible describes him as pretty scrawny. He probably didn't consume much protein powder or spend a lot of time in the weight room. All he saw when he looked in the mirror was a skinny guy hiding in a cave.

I'm not sure if you've noticed, but our world is obsessed with status, titles, and labels. We often try to define other people with categories related to beauty, body shape, ethnicity, occupation, net worth, height, weight, age, academic pedigree, salary, job title, and so much more. If we're not careful, we may be tempted to base our own identity on such labels.

No man-made label has the power to define your soul. God is the one who created you, and He alone has the right to tell you who you really are. Once you find your significance in Him, everything else comes into focus.

Gideon questioned the angel's message because Gideon had assumed that if God was as powerful as He claimed to be, He wouldn't have allowed Gideon and his people to live in fear and chaos. Gideon had to wrestle with his faith before he could embrace his true identity in the Lord. Maybe you've had a difficult time trusting God for the same reasons Gideon was struggling. Perhaps you look at the heartbreak in your life and think to yourself, "Well, if there's really a God, then I guess He's either too weak to change my situation or He's too indifferent to care."

The truth is that God is right by your side, just like He was right there with Gideon. God had allowed the situation to turn bleak before He intervened—but He never left Gideon's side. He was always with Him.

Sometimes, God will allow us to experience trials for a time so that we gain a deeper understanding of how much we truly need Him. I believe God often lets a situation get worse just to make room for a bigger miracle. I have experienced this in my own life, time and time again. Though I didn't love going through the struggle at the time, those moments of turmoil caused me to see God more clearly as my loving Father. I felt the presence of the Holy Spirit as my ever-present comforter, and I grew in my relationship with Jesus, my merciful Savior.

Gideon eventually did prove to be the mighty warrior God created him to be. You can be the mighty warrior He created *you* to be, too! Though this manifests differently in each individual's life, God has a purpose and a plan for you that only you can fulfill (Philippians 4:13). God looks at you and proclaims you are a masterpiece (Ephesians 2:10)! He says you are a new creation in Christ (2 Corinthians 5:17). He says you are His child (Galatians 3:26). He says you are loved (John 3:16).

Don't let the labels of this world stick to you or change your thinking (Romans 12:2). God has labeled you as loved, and His opinion of you is the only one that counts.

Dave

When I hear the story of Gideon, it makes me imagine the theme music from the *Rocky* movie training montages (which still get me pumped up). I was a child of the 1980s. I'll bet you're already getting flashbacks of bulked up action figures, leg warmers, Cabbage Patch Kids, and big hair. It was quite a decade. I grew up on movies like *Back to the Future, Top Gun, The Goonies,* and my personal favorite—*The Karate Kid.*

If you've never seen *The Karate Kid,* the plot follows a teenage kid named Daniel who wants to learn karate so he can defend himself from local bullies. He meets a mysterious older man named Mr. Miyagi, who turns out to be a karate master. They form a friendship, and Daniel eventually begs Mr. Miyagi to teach him karate. Mr. Miyagi agrees, on the condition that Daniel follows his instructions *no matter what.* No questions asked.

Daniel agrees and shows up for his first day of lessons. But instead of teaching him karate, Mr. Miyagi tells Daniel to wax all of his cars. Daniel has to do it with a very specific, circular motion, applying the wax with one hand and removing it with the other. By the end of the day, Daniel's arms and shoulders are hurting badly, but he doesn't complain. He shows up the next morning, certain that this will be the day he finally learns karate. Instead, Mr. Miyagi tells him to paint the fence. He has to paint it with a specific, continuous, up-and-down motion to prevent streaking in the paint.

After several days of forced labor, Daniel finally snaps. He confronts his teacher and accuses him of making him a slave instead of teaching him karate. Mr. Miyagi says, "I have been teaching you karate this entire time. Show me how to wax the car. Show me how to paint the fence."

As Daniel begins to mimic the motions from those tasks, Mr. Miyagi begins to throw a flurry of punches and kicks at Daniel, which, to Daniel's amazement, he is able to block. Daniel's body had been learning karate even though Daniel didn't realize it.

Mr. Miyagi bows to his student, and in that moment, something clicked in my head.

For me, that wasn't just a moment of Hollywood magic; it was a moment when some truths of God's Word came to life in real and practical ways.

There are times in life when I feel like I'm begging God to reveal His will. All I'm doing is toiling away at some mundane, repetitive task, just waiting for my life to begin. But what I've come to realize through the years is that God doesn't waste anything. He's always teaching us, always shaping us. He's preparing us to respond instinctively to the battles of life with a level of faith and skill we didn't know we possessed.

It's the same for you! You're on your way to becoming a spiritual black belt, and your heavenly Father is with you every step of the way!

Whether you're in a season with a flabby belly or with rock solid abs, keep taking steps toward health and supporting your spouse in his or her health journey. Remember that physical health is important, but our physical bodies are temporary. Don't get obsessed with your physical health at the expense of your spiritual health or your family. Find a balanced approach to be at your best and give yourself some grace along the way. Even on the days when you feel weak and inadequate, remember that you are a warrior.

CHAPTER 5:

In Sickness and in Health

Ashley

One of Jesus' most famous teachings centers around the concept of what it truly means to love your neighbor. In Luke 10:25, a teacher of the religious law asked Jesus what to do to inherit eternal life. Jesus, in His customary style, initially answered the question with another question. He asked the teacher to take a shot at answering.

The teacher said that the most important law was to love the Lord God with all your heart, mind, soul, and strength and then to love your neighbor as yourself. Jesus congratulated him on knowing the correct answer all along. But this teacher was apparently very concerned about his own image and ego, so he wanted to justify asking the question in the first place. He threw out a follow-up question: "Who is my neighbor?"

Jesus replied with a story about a traveler taking the dangerous road from Jerusalem to Jericho, where crime rates were on the rise and the terrain was treacherous. This poor traveler fell into the hands of bandits, who robbed and beat him before leaving him for dead. The poor man was helpless and unconscious at the side of the road when a priest came upon him, but this pious passerby didn't want to get his hands dirty, so he just kept walking. A second religious leader also came by but also was too busy or too indifferent to stop and help.

Then a third person passed by, and he happened to be a Samaritan. While telling this story, Jesus was speaking to a Jewish audience. They had deep-seated, generational prejudices against people from Samaria. Samaritans were considered to be on the lowest rung on the societal ladder. Jews had been raised to have nothing at all to do with them, and now Jesus was introducing a despised Samaritan as the hero of His parable.

The Samaritan in the story rushed to aid the injured Jewish man. He bandaged his wounds and carried him to his own donkey before transporting the victim to an inn to recover. The Samaritan then promised the innkeeper he would return and assume all financial responsibility for the injured man's expenses. In that day and time, this was a scandalous story. As Jesus completed the parable of the good Samaritan, He asked the teacher of the Jewish religious law which of the three passersby had been a "neighbor" to the victim. The bewildered man had to give credit to the Samaritan—the only one who stopped to help. Jesus agreed and told his listeners to be that kind of neighbor.

Over the past two thousand years, this simple story has been the inspiration for multiple charities, hospitals, and laws designed to heal and protect the wounded and powerless. Whether Jesus told this story as a real encounter or simply as a metaphor to illustrate a real truth is up for debate. But either way, the lesson is clear. We are called to love our neighbors, and one simple, selfless act of love has the power to change a life.

You might be wondering why I'm sharing the story of The Good Samaritan in a chapter on loving your spouse in sickness and in health. I'm sharing it because your spouse is your closest neighbor. Your spouse is the person for whom you should make the greatest sacrifices. When your spouse is ill or injured, you should be the first to spring into action and the last one to leave their side.

Dave

In our fast-paced culture, we're all tempted to chase stuff that doesn't really matter. We're conditioned to value possessions over people, but people must always take priority over all other pursuits. I firmly believe that God created love to be the centerpiece of life. There's no higher purpose on earth than to love and to be loved. Sometimes love can be seen most clearly in the example of couples who are loving each other through a season of physical illness.

My mom served as a hospice nurse for many years, and as a kid I would tag along on some of her home visits. Spending time with dying people forever changed my perspective on love and life. I discovered that when a person knows his or her time on earth is short, what matters most comes into focus more clearly than ever before.

These dying patients—whether young or old, black or white, male or female, educated or illiterate—shared remarkably similar end-of-life priorities. They valued faith, family, and friendships. Their relationships were all that mattered. In short, they cared most about love. Every joy they treasured in those final moments was related to love, and every regret that tormented them was tied to a failure to give or receive love.

The key to a purpose-filled, regret-free life starts with a deeper understanding of love. Living well begins with loving well. I'm reminded of this powerful principle when I see the courage of our friends John and Dawn. John and Dawn are an amazing married couple. They laugh together, they dream together, they support each other, and on top of all that, their names even rhyme! They're the kind of people who light up a room the moment they walk through the door.

John has enjoyed a great deal of success in the corporate world and Dawn has devoted much of her time and energy to philanthropy. They both are extremely talented and also generous with their time, expertise, and resources. The world is truly a better place because of them both. They've always had big dreams and big plans for the future. But a few years ago, those plans changed in a way they never could've expected.

When Dawn was in her mid-forties, half-way through the life she had mapped out in her mind, this happy couple was dealt a devastating blow. Though Dawn was healthy and vibrant, her doctor gave her news that would rock them to the core. She was diagnosed with Multiple Sclerosis, a debilitating and life-limiting illness.

This stopped John and Dawn in their tracks. Their plans for the future instantly and irreversibly changed. This diagnosis was going to be the biggest test their faith and their marriage had ever experienced. And though these past few years have been incredibly challenging for them both, I've stood in awe at their faith in God and their love for one another as they've beautifully lived out the vow, *"in sickness and in health."*

Slowly and systematically, the disease has robbed Dawn of her physical vibrancy and freedoms. She is now confined to a wheelchair. The tedious process of preparing to leave the house has gone from fifteen minutes when she was healthy to an ordeal that can now last five hours or more. Through it all, despite shedding many tears, they've never given up on each other.

The tenderness with which John cares for her physical needs is awe-inspiring, and the way Dawn affirms John is beautiful. The faith they both have in God is unshakable. They stand in faith, knowing

God's promises are true. Even if physical healing doesn't happen in this lifetime, eternal healing will come through faith in Christ.

In the meantime, they face each day together. The disease may be Dawn's diagnosis, but the struggle belongs to them both. Watching them courageously face this struggle together, completely united, has inspired me and countless others. I pray God would continue to give them strength and grace for the road ahead, and I pray that if Ashley and I ever face a similar challenge, we'll have the faith to face it like John and Dawn!

Ashley

Sickness can run the gamut from a simple cold to a life-threatening illness. In either scenario, we have an opportunity to show great love, kindness, and patience to our spouse. The longer the illness lasts, the harder this becomes. We have seen the hardship of a serious illness nearly destroy the love and respect between a couple. We have also seen couples come together with tremendous love, faith, and unity to support one another and overcome the destructive nature of an illness, regardless of whether physical healing ever occurs.

Some of you might be fighting a major disease right now. My heart and prayers go out to you and your family. No matter what the doctors or test results tell you, I want you to know that there is hope. I love these Bible verses that poignantly speak to this issue:

> *Two are better than one,*
> *because they have a good return for their labor:*
> *If either of them falls down, one can help the other up.*
> *But pity anyone who falls*
> *and has no one to help them up.*
> *Also, if two lie down together, they will keep warm.*

But how can one keep warm alone?
Though one may be overpowered,
two can defend themselves.
A cord of three strands is not quickly broken.
(Ecclesiastes 4:9-12)

As husband and wife, we are going to experience various trials throughout our marriage—many that we never see coming. However dire it may appear, we must choose to come together and help one another. God gave us a great gift in one another, and He is with us. This "cord of three strands," as described in the verse above, is you, your spouse, and God. There is tremendous hope when all three are tightly intertwined.

Whether you are going through a season of illness right now or you both are currently healthy, here are seven important things to do when your spouse is sick:

1. Acknowledge the illness.

When your spouse is sick, the worst thing you can do is act like the illness doesn't exist. You must acknowledge the pain they are in and the fear your spouse might be experiencing when facing a major illness. Stay close and offer encouragement, but also realize that the only way the two of you can fight the illness is to first address that it exists, that times are uncertain and scary, and that this season of ailment is tough.

2. Be there.

If at all possible, try to accompany your spouse to all the major appointments, especially if your spouse has requested that you be there. Occasionally it might not make sense to you and the timing of the appointment might be inconvenient, but you still need to do it. Your physical presence can bring your spouse peace. You can be there to physically take care of your spouse, pray with them, hold their hand, console them, and even cry with him or her when facing bad test results.

We need to be present to remind our spouse how much we love them and that we aren't going to leave their side during this struggle.

3. Lighten the load.

When a person faces a dangerous upcoming surgery or intense treatment, the ensuing fear and anxiety can be overwhelming. No matter which spouse is going through the illness, it can affect both of you. If you are the "healthy" spouse, try to bear the load of your family's daily duties as much as possible to help lighten your partner's load.

When he or she is having a particularly hard day with pain, fear, and sadness, offer to take your spouse out of the house. Sometimes we just need to create a diversion—like going to a movie, eating lunch at their favorite restaurant, or taking a walk outside to get some fresh air. It's okay to laugh together in the midst of this hardship. Laughter and smiles are good for the soul! Other times, we just need to listen...to their concerns, fears, details about the surgery or treatment, and anything else that may be on their mind.

Whatever you do, your willingness to jump in and ease their burden will help your spouse to face this trial without being overtaken by the weight of it all.

4. Honor their requests.

In an age of social media, we can let the entire world know about every little detail of our lives with a few clicks on the computer. Facebook and Instagram are a great place to ask for prayers and make others aware of needs. However, it's important to consult with your spouse first.

A few years ago, a friend of ours received a breast cancer diagnosis, and the couple decided to only tell family and a few friends about it. They did this in part because they didn't want too many people showing up at the hospital or making unannounced drop-ins at their house. They also decided to be discreet because the wife didn't want to share her diagnosis with people at work. She wasn't going against work policy or anything underhanded. She just didn't want her colleagues to treat her differently because they felt sorry for her. She wanted to keep working as long as she could, and her job was one aspect of her life that could feel "normal" during a long health battle.

Her husband honored those wishes. He kept the news within their close circle of friends and family, and she was able to continue working while getting chemo treatments on extended lunch breaks until she achieved remission. She even found a wig that matched her hair, so when it started falling out due to the treatment, she could continue to go to work and about her daily life without a beat.

She faced cancer how *she* wanted to face cancer—with her husband, kids, family, and close friends walking through it alongside her. Those outside her inner circle were none the wiser.

This may sound harsh to some of you, but I get it. Sometimes we want to put the news out there and accept others' help and prayers, but other times we just want those closest to us to know. Neither is right or wrong; it is simply a preference. Whether your spouse wants to share their diagnosis widely or would like to only share the news with close family and friends, it is important to be sensitive to what your spouse requests during this season.

5. Ask for help.

This is especially important when you are going through a long health battle with your spouse. Cancer treatments, for instance, can last for months and even years. In order to maintain a job, family life, and some sense of normalcy, you are going to need help.

We must resist the urge to be prideful and think we can face all these challenges alone. We need to reach out to friends and family we trust. Sometimes that means hiring a reliable babysitter, nurse, or cleaning person who can help out during this time. There is no shame in that at all. In fact, the "extra hands" will allow you to spend more time with your spouse.

Like I mentioned above, your spouse might be resistant to reaching out for help out of a desire to be discreet, so it is important to talk to your spouse about *what* kind of help would lighten the load, *whom* they are comfortable asking, and *when* the help would be most beneficial to them and the family.

6. Talk about it.

Being in a house or hospital, day in and day out, with a very ill spouse can certainly take a toll on your mind and heart. It's important that we have "safe" people in our lives with whom we can talk about what we are going through. This person can be a same-gender friend, counselor, pastor, or family member. He or she must be someone you can trust with the details of the illness as well as your feelings. This confidant must also be someone who encourages you and shares your faith. Apart from a parent or sibling, it is also important that this safe person is the same gender as you. This protect you against temptation and inappropriate relationships that could be harmful to your marriage.

7. Pray about it.

This might be the most important one of all. So much is unknown when we face a serious illness. We need the power of God in our lives. He is our ultimate Healer. He can give us peace that surpasses understanding and a calm in the unpredictable storm. As spouses, we need to pray together *and* on our own. Pray for healing, peace, strength, good news, effective medicine, successful surgeries, and support. God hears our prayers and calms our hearts.

More than anything, we need to realize that this crisis is an opportunity to honor our marital vow to love each other "in sickness and in health." God can use this season of illness to strengthen our marriage and our faith if we don't lose hope and stay strong together.

Dave

My friends Freddy and Linda have a remarkable marriage, but you wouldn't know just how remarkable by looking at the surface. On Freddy's skull, there are some deep scars. Those scars tell a story of redemption, love, and the power of a wife who vowed to love her husband in sickness and in health—and really meant it.

Several years back, Freddy suffered a traumatic brain injury that rendered him nearly incapacitated. He couldn't speak, and he could do nothing for himself. For over a year, Linda was his sole caregiver. She loved and cared for him with a compassion that melted the hearts of all who saw them together. It was a difficult time for her, but her commitment to him was unshakable.

After a year of round-the-clock caregiving, the impossible happened. If you don't believe in modern-day miracles, it's probably because you haven't met Freddy. Against all odds and doctors' dire predictions, Freddy began to emerge from his catatonic state and regain his mental and physical capacity.

Today, Freddy is as sharp as ever, and he and Linda are some of the most faithful leaders in our church. Freddy, who was helpless a few short years ago, is now able to serve and support Linda through a challenging season in her own life. Their partnership, faith, and commitment to each other is a wonderful picture of what marriage can and should be.

I'm not sure what terminology the doctors used to make sense of Freddy's remarkable recovery. There are probably some big, fancy, scientific terms used to demystify the miracle. For me, I think it's all a result of love. Freddy is a walking miracle and a testament to love's healing power—God's everlasting love and Linda's steadfast commitment to love Freddy through his traumatic brain injury.

Ashley has a beautiful saying that always makes me think of Freddy and Linda. Ashley says, "A strong marriage rarely has two strong people at the same time. It is a husband and wife who take turns being strong for each other in the moments when the other feels weak."

That's really the key to loving your spouse "in sickness and in health." Be there for each other, serve each other, cherish the time you have together, and take turns being strong for each other. If you'll do these things, your marriage will become stronger than any illness or setback that comes your way.

CHAPTER 6:

Healthy Food

Dave

I'm going to start out the chapter on food by sharing a story that has nothing to do with food. This isn't just because I have an undiagnosed case of ADHD (although, I might). It's because the story is about having clear goals and one of the most important aspects of winning with food is in having clear goals and clear motivation.

I remember the feelings of joy and anticipation when I was ready to purchase an engagement ring for Ashley. I was a college student, and I was poor in a way that only college students can understand. I was broke, but I was in love, and love always finds a way! Ashley understood my lack of resources and would have happily married me without an engagement ring, but I wanted to give one to her. I realized that this simple piece of jewelry wasn't just a culturally enforced tradition perpetuated by jewelers; it was an opportunity to express my love and commitment to my future bride in a way that would bring a huge smile to her face. I knew it would also create a tangible reminder of this season of our journey together. In addition to that, it would get me in the habit of self-sacrifice for the sake of my bride, which is a vital habit for any healthy marriage!

After doing some research on the cut and clarity of diamonds, I felt ready to go shopping. It wasn't long before I was in the mall jewelry store holding the perfect ring. The only problem was that I didn't have any money. Luckily, they had a layaway program where I could have ninety days to make payments on it, and when the last payment was made, I could come by the store and pick it up. They say, "A diamond is forever." I'm not sure if that's true, but for a long time, I thought the payments would last forever!

Ninety days sounded like a lot of time to my young mind, but a few days in, I hadn't made any money and I started calculating how much income I'd need to average per day to pay off the ring in time. I knew I needed to take quick action, so I started applying for jobs anywhere I could. The minimum wage I'd been making on campus as part of the landscaping crew wasn't going to cut it, so I looked for server jobs or sales jobs or anything that might produce more income.

Though it's not my nature to walk into a place and ask for a job, love had made me fearless. I boldly walked up to one potential employer after another with my résumé in hand, but over and over the answer was no. I was discouraged but undaunted. I finally landed what I thought would be a perfect job as a server for a high-end hotel restaurant, but I rushed my way through the personality profile thinking it was only a formality. It turns out the personality profile was more important than I thought, and I actually failed it.

I didn't think it was even possible to fail a personality profile, but somehow, I did. That's right. You're reading a book co-written by a guy who couldn't pass a test that many convicted felons working at the same place had easily passed. It was not my proudest moment. My friend, Smitty, later went to work at that place, and for years afterward, he would introduce me to his coworkers as "the guy who failed the personality profile."

From what I can tell, I became something of an urban legend at the restaurant as the only guy who had ever failed the test. I didn't dwell on the blow to my pride for too long, though, because I didn't have time. There were only eighty-three days left to pay off this ring, and I quickly had to figure out a way to do it.

I weighed my options and pulled out my phone to call up an old friend who managed an electronics store. I wasn't any good with electronics. In fact, I barely knew how to operate my cell phone (and this was back before the phones were even "smart").

I opted not to tell him that I was electronically illiterate and that I had just flunked a personality profile. I figured I could get past my technology deficiencies by working hard and leaning heavily on my people skills to make up the difference. I explained that I was highly motivated because I had a limited window of time to pay for a ring for a girl who was way out of my league, and I wanted to seal the deal as fast as I could. My friend graciously agreed to give me a shot, and I was on the job the next day.

The learning curve at the new job was even steeper than I had anticipated, but my resolve had never been stronger. I studied harder than I'd studied for any class I'd ever taken in school. I wasn't just working for a good grade; I was working for my future bride. I was picturing the smile on her face when I put that ring on her finger. I was imagining her saying "Yes!" and jumping into my arms. I was picturing the scene of telling our future children and grandchildren the story of how I'd proposed and what her response had been. I was working for much more than just a diamond. I was working for the opportunity to create a timeless moment, a moment that would lead to a lifelong journey with the one I loved.

After hundreds of hours, scores of cell phone sales, dozens of training manuals, and a lot of hard work, I finally had enough money to pay off the ring. On day eighty-eight of the ninety-day layaway, I proudly marched to the cashier of the jewelry store and made my final payment. I ransomed that beautiful little ring and held it in my hands like I'd just climbed on a podium to receive an Olympic gold medal!

I was able to persevere through all the work because my goal was so clear. I knew what I had to do, and I was motivated by love. If you want to win with food, the principles are surprisingly similar. In all aspects of your health, you have to set clear goals. You have to know the source of your motivation. Until you do, you'll be setting yourself up for failure. Once you define your goals and your motivation, you will be unstoppable!

Ashley

When Dave popped the question and showed me the absolutely beautiful ring that he'd worked so hard to get just for me, I was utterly speechless! In fact, my first response was, "Nuh-uh! Nuh-uh! No way!" As you can imagine, poor Dave was extremely nervous and was pretty confused by my initial response. So, I quickly said, "Yes! Yes! Of course, I will marry you!" I knew that I had hit the jackpot with Dave, and I couldn't wait to marry him.

Dave and I met at Georgetown College, a small liberal arts Christian college in Georgetown, KY. Once we started dating, we were inseparable. We would often stay up until the wee hours of the morning watching movies and eating pizza—along with other unhealthy snacks—in the communal area of his frat house. We were (and still are) so in love and happy that we would lose track of time...and calories. So much so that it started showing on the scale and in our energy levels.

One night, Dave excitedly introduced me to the *Rocky* movies with Sylvester Stallone. They are some of his very favorite movies, so he was like a kid at Christmas. Not to mention, his fraternity nickname was literally "Sly," after the handsome movie star himself.

We ordered an extra-large pizza—just for the two of us, mind you—and began our *Rocky* movie marathon. By the end of the first movie, we had eaten the *entire pizza*, and my stomach felt stuffed. Dave felt a little sick, too. Between the Coke and the pizza, we had overindulged. I looked down at my protruding belly and thought about how I needed to change my eating habits, or I was going to feel terrible on my wedding day.

I knew I needed a plan and that I couldn't do it on my own. So I told Dave how I was feeling and asked him if he'd be up for committing to a health/fitness contract with me. He was intrigued. I told him how I absolutely loved staying up late with him and indulging in our favorite foods, but I also explained how it wasn't making me feel great. I wanted to look and feel my very best on our wedding day, and I certainly wanted to feel sexy on our wedding night. I think that was the statement that really got Dave's attention. He perked right up and said, "Yeah. You're right. We need to be healthier to look and feel our best not only for our wedding night but also for our overall health. Let's do this!"

So, like all contracts, we knew we needed to put our plan in writing, but we couldn't find any paper close by at the time. The only thing we had to write on was our empty, greasy pizza box. Go figure! We laughed at the prospect but then felt like it was the perfect place to write down our plan. We crafted a simple plan:

1. We would stop eating late at night.
2. We would start eating fewer carbs and more protein and veggies.

3. We would exercise five days a week for at least 30 minutes at a time (either together or on our own).

Pretty basic, right? However, basic doesn't mean easy, or none of us would have any weight issues. Sticking to a fitness/food plan is hard, and that is precisely why Dave and I decided to write down our expectations and sign this contract.

We made this contract as a means to hold ourselves and one another accountable, and it worked! I ended up getting certified to teach aerobics and taught classes regularly on campus, and Dave started running again. We also traded our late-night pizza and movie nights for a midnight Tae Bo class at Dave's frat house. It was so fun, and we even had some friends join us!

When it came to our healthy eating plan, we realized that there were a lot of healthy options at the campus cafeteria (or "caf," as we liked to call it). I frequently ate healthy meals like rotisserie chicken, steamed broccoli, and brown rice. It was delicious! I also allowed myself some little indulgences from time to time. My favorite was the caf's famous pecan pie—so good!

Over the course of three months, Dave and I started toning up and feeling much better. Our energy levels were higher than they had ever been, and we were both so ready for our wedding day... and night. We accomplished our goal, and it felt so good!

You and your spouse can do the same, but it will take both of you being on board and committing to stay the course—especially when it comes to your healthy eating plan. It will also take both of you resisting the urge to point fingers at one another when one isn't keeping the plan as much as the other. As spouses, we hold each other accountable best when we lead with encouragement rather than accusations. Dave certainly did this for me when I was having an "off" day, and he continues to do so decades later. As we've shared earlier, we have gained and lost weight a lot through our marriage, but we have been able to reclaim and maintain a healthy eating plan because we keep encouraging one another to be the healthiest version of ourselves. We keep pressing forward towards a healthier, holier, and happier life together—through thick and thin (wink, wink).

Dave

I love food, but food doesn't always love me back. After my initial thyroid diagnosis, I wanted to start reclaiming some power over my body in a healthy way. So, I decided to go full force into a lifestyle change. I started with my diet. Even though I had always been pretty disciplined in my exercising from my early years in martial arts to my consistent running and weightlifting, I had typically been pretty undisciplined in my diet. I worked out primarily because I liked eating, and I used my workouts as an excuse to sabotage my health by justifying an unhealthy diet.

All my research was pointing to the power of a healthy diet in combatting thyroid issues. I ran internet searches on food and thyroid conditions until my eyeballs felt like they were going to dry up and fall out of my head. I half expected my eyes to actually fall out since the rest of my body seemed to be falling apart, too.

Thankfully, my eyes stayed in place. I actually got Lasik (laser eye surgery) to make my vision 20/20 without glasses for the first time in my life. In the midst of all this, my eyesight was ironically the one part of my body that had been improving while everything else seemed to be falling apart. It gave me a psychological advantage to pursue measurable improvement in other areas which made the Lasik well worth the investment. It's also the reason I'm able to type out these words on a laptop without wearing any glasses.

I'm thankful that my eyes work, but that's really not what this chapter is about. I'm talking about food, which has always been one of the most enjoyable parts of my life. I've had a lifelong love affair with food. Like a dysfunctional relationship, I'd often run to food for comfort, but then I'd experience a lot of digestive discomfort as a result. It tasted good going down, but then it started a nuclear war once it reached my stomach and intestines.

As much as I loved my junk food, I knew something had to change. I decided to make drastic and disciplined actions to reimagine my diet. I experimented with Veganism (even though I love meat and animal products). When that short-lived experiment failed, I started eating animal products but still trying to eat clean. I was also researching specific foods that helped.

I practically had a funeral for beloved foods like Doritos that I was now banning from my pantry. It was a period of actual grieving when I thought about going through the rest of my life without many of the processed foods that had literally become such a part of me. If we truly "are what we eat," then I was at least 60% Doritos, pizzas and microwaveable burritos. I knew that if I was going to feel my best, I needed to make some big changes and "break up" with certain foods that were sabotaging my progress.

Something called "bone broth" kept popping up in my Google searches as a good combatant to thyroid issues. I bought some and force myself to drink a warm mug full of it every day. Honestly, it was disgusting. It left me with an aftertaste that made me want to barf for the rest of the day. (I've always wanted to include the word *barf* in a book, so thank you for helping me with this "bucket list" item.)

I gave up on the bone broth. I also gave up on some of my other radical dietary experiments. In surrender, I decided that I'd rather live with stomach pain or even die young than spend the rest of my life guzzling bone broth and eating tofu instead of steak. I relapsed back into my unhealthy diet, but now I couldn't even enjoy the food, because I ate it with the guilt and shame that I had failed in my goals. This was one of the many setbacks I experienced in the early days of my journey.

Ultimately, I finally settled into a sustainable balance. I realized that "sustainability" was really the goal, because no diet was really going to work if I didn't have the will to maintain it for a lifetime. I had to find something I could do and keep doing. I also had to give myself a lot of grace to stop beating myself up when I fell short.

After a lot of trial and error, I finally found a rhythm that works for me. I freed myself from the prison of thinking I had to follow anybody else's strict, prescribed plan of dieting. I certainly learned from experts, but I had to find what works best for me even if it looks different from what others are doing. Through trial and error, I found which foods I should eat more often, which ones I should eat less often, and what I should probably avoid altogether.

The biggest dietary changes I've made, which have been sustainable and helpful, have been the following:

1. Limiting dairy products and typically using almond milk instead of regular milk. I still eat cheese occasionally, but not nearly as much dairy as I used to eat. I've learned the hard way that too much dairy messes with me.
2. Limiting red meat and eating less meat in general. I love red meat, but the less I eat, the better I feel.
3. Drinking low-sugar protein shakes, which keeps my energy up with plenty of protein but without a sugar crash or the stomach pain that can happen with eating too much meat.

4. Taking a daily vitamin and other supplements, including a daily fiber supplement which helps with digestive health and lowers cholesterol. This is one of the cheapest and easiest ways to stay healthy.

5. Limiting sugar while still giving myself room to splurge occasionally, plus finding sweet foods I can enjoy daily. I was addicted to ice cream—and I'll still have real ice cream occasionally—but more often I've switched to a lower-sugar frozen yogurt or ice cream made from coconut milk, which has no dairy. Put a little reduced-sugar chocolate syrup on it and you won't even know it's almost "healthy."

6. Intermittent fasting. This one has been HUGE. During my most disciplined streak of doing this, I was only eating in an eight-hour window, from 8 a.m. until 4 p.m. Other than a cup of coffee or sugar-free popsicle at night, I didn't eat anything after 4pm. When I was sticking to this plan, I dropped twenty pounds in a two-month period and I felt amazing. It proved not to be completely sustainable as a lifelong habit, so I now do it periodically. In general, I try to stop eating early in the evening, which helps my system reset. I highly recommend intermittent fasting as a way to kickstart weight loss and digestive health, or as an ongoing lifestyle if you can stick with it.

7. Allowing some "cheat days," when I eat like I'm in college again and keep some antacid on hand to help minimize the "food hangover." These free days can't happen all the time, but allowing yourself some freedom makes the overall lifestyle change much more sustainable.

You don't have to try to mimic my own plan. You have to find what works best for you. Some things I've outlined on my list might be positive and life-changing for you, or maybe your list is ultimately going to look completely different from mine. Be willing to learn from other people and be willing to explore some trial and error, but ultimately, you've got to find a food plan that is sustainable, enjoyable and most importantly, works for *you*. Even in our marriage, Ashley and I have learned to support each other in whatever is working for us as individuals, without pressuring each other to follow "our" diet plan.

Food is going to be a big part of this journey toward a healthy life. Food is a big part of life, and it should be an *enjoyable* part of life. Don't let the "enjoyable" part die just because you're trying to get healthier. You might have to get a bit more creative and disciplined than you were with food in the past, but you can still enjoy it more than ever if you'll keep working until you find what works best with your body.

Even after you've found a plan that seems to work, don't get stuck. Your body isn't static. It's going to keep changing. What works right now might not work next year. Be flexible enough to keep pivoting. Keep listening to your body. Keep being willing to try new things to maximize your health and quality of life. If you're willing to keep doing this, then food can be an ongoing source of enjoyment instead of an ongoing source of stress.

Ashley

It's impossible to have a comprehensive conversation about health without talking about food. In our own marriage, food has been a great source of comfort and connection for us, but it has also been a temptation to slip into unhealthy habits. We didn't want this chapter to be about recipes or grocery shopping lists because, as Dave mentioned before, a healthy eating plan needs to be specific to what works best and is sustainable for you, individually and collectively. However, we do want to share some of the many ways that food has shaped our own health journey.

Throughout our marriage, my weight and healthy lifestyle have fluctuated a bit. Any time I was stressed out, just had a baby, was enjoying eating without thinking—or all of those things at the same time—I would eventually realize that I needed to get back into shape. I would immediately go tell Dave about my desire to get healthier, as if he was going to be as excited and motivated as I was.

Regardless, he always told me that he thought I looked beautiful just the way I was, but he would support me in any way he could. That was exactly what I needed to hear. It is amazing the difference a spouse can make in another spouse's journey to lose weight or simply lead a healthier lifestyle.

Over the years, Dave has played a key role in my quest to get fit. I don't think I could have reached any of my health goals without him. As spouses, we can choose to help or hinder our partners in this effort. But, honestly, don't we *all* want our mates to be healthy? Sure, we do!

Here a few steps a spouse can take to help his or her partner reach their fitness goals:

1. Share in your spouse's excitement for the journey ahead.

When one spouse wants to lose weight, but the other is totally happy with "how things are," the climate at home can become a little tricky. Change is hard! However, leading a healthier life is a good thing that we need to encourage. We want our spouse to look and feel better, so we need to share in their excitement. When I was doing Weight Watchers, I would text Dave about my weekly weight loss after I weighed in, and he would send the sweetest text back to congratulate me and recognize the hard work I had put into that week. It always meant so much to me that he shared my excitement, and it propelled me to work hard the next week.

2. Help your partner manage the schedule to make time for exercise or meal planning.

If we want our spouse to be at their best, then we need to help make our family schedule more conducive to leading a healthy lifestyle. If your spouse is motivated to attend a Zumba® class several times during the week, then offer to take the kids to their practices on those days. If your spouse has a running buddy who can run around the neighborhood with them a few mornings a week, then take over the breakfast routine with the kids on those mornings. The main idea here is to help and be flexible when adjusting to the changes.

3. Join your spouse.

What's better than the first two goals? Well, deciding to *join* your partner in the journey to better health, of course! Do that new workout with your spouse. Help with buying and cooking healthier food, and here's a crazy thought—*eat* the healthy food. You might even like it.

I know countless couples that have decided to do various Beachbody® workouts and food plans together right before a big event. It's fun to take the "before" and "after" photos to see your progress. And, who knows? It might just stick for one or even both of you. Again, you have to find what works best for you.

Dave and I have tried different video workout programs before, but the one thing that seems to work for us during this season of our life is going to the gym. We attend the local YMCA and love it. When we first get there, we put the kids in the childcare (included in the membership, which is a *huge* plus), and then we have a cup of coffee before working out.

It might sound weird, but it's kind of like a minidate when we have that coffee. We only take about fifteen to twenty minutes, but in that short time, we help get each other motivated for the day ahead. For me, it's like a big blast of fresh air in my face before "getting my sweat on." I love it, and I always have a better workout when Dave is there to have coffee with me. There's something special about sipping a little joe and staring into his deep, dark eyes that gets me going. I love going to the gym together, and it has certainly helped me to stay motivated.

4. Affirm your spouse with encouraging words and compliments.

Who doesn't love to be told that you look healthier or have lost weight? I can't hear it enough! Words are powerful, and a spouse's words carry even more weight. We need to take the time to notice the positive changes that our mate is making—in their bodies, their food choices, their exercise, or whatever the case may be. Tell your husband that you are proud of how disciplined he has been with his healthier food choices. Tell your wife that she looks amazing in her favorite jeans. Grab his arms, and gush over those "guns." Embrace her, and comment on how toned she feels, and tell her how she exudes confidence and strength. If your partner didn't meet their goal for that week, offer a word of encouragement to keep them motivated. Don't hold back. Keep the compliments and encouragement coming.

5. Celebrate the "wins" with something tangible.

It is extremely important that we celebrate with our spouse when they have reached a goal. It's motivating when we can decide how we are going to celebrate before the goal has been attained. Whether big or small, it gives our partner something to look forward to and helps them to stay focused. Maybe it's a massage, a pedicure, a new outfit, a nice dinner, or even a cruise (if it's a really big goal). Make it fun and exciting. Hard work should be rewarded and celebrated. There's nothing better than celebrating the achievement of meeting your health goals together.

Dave

Friend, you and your spouse can craft a healthy eating plan that works for you both individually and together. Changing our eating habits can be difficult and even frustrating, so don't forget to give yourself some freedom in all this. Having a plan is important. However, remember that a plan doesn't have to be a prison. Yes, I miss eating Doritos as much as I used to, but I still eat Doritos sometimes. They seem even more delicious now than they used to be. I still have slight love handles, and I'm okay with that. Abs are overrated. Any diet plan has to have some flexibility built in. Enjoy all things in moderation, and remember: You and your spouse are in this together.

CHAPTER 7:

Healthy Sex

Ashley

On our podcast, *The Naked Marriage*, Dave and I recently interviewed our friends Tyler and Alyssa Gordon. They courageously shared a story of childhood trauma that sent chills up my spine, broke my heart into pieces, and brought tears to my eyes. It's a story of unspeakable suffering followed by miraculous healing.

Alyssa and her sister, Kayla, had grown up at our church. They were there almost every Sunday along with their mom and stepdad. On the surface, they looked like a picture-perfect family. Behind closed doors, however, Alyssa and Kayla were living in a secret hell.

Alyssa shared that, from the time she was nine years old until he moved out when she was seventeen, her stepfather had been brutally abusing her. He ruled over her with terror, threatening to kill her if she ever told anyone about his repugnant sexual crimes against her. As Alyssa progressed through her early teenage years, not only did the rape continue, but he even began pimping her out to his friends.

She was forced to do whatever these evil men told her to do. If she ever resisted in any way, she was beaten and terrorized. Her stepfather was an evil man. He played the part of a loving father in public, but behind closed doors, he was inflicting despicable acts of physical, emotional, and sexual abuse.

As Alyssa shared her harrowing story, she talked honestly about how heartbreaking it was during those years of abuse to feel that her prayers were being unanswered. God was the only one who saw the pain she was enduring. She cried out to Him daily in her prayers, but during her eight years of suffering, those prayers felt unanswered. As her mind, body and innocence were being ravaged by evil men, her faith was being tested as well. She continued to pray, but she would also ask herself the obvious question, "How could an all-powerful and loving God see what I'm going through and do nothing to intervene?"

It's questions like this and experiences like hers that have caused many people to lose faith over the years. The truth is, there aren't any Christian clichés or platitudes that can neatly explain away the devastating pain of people like Alyssa. Trying to minimize a person's deepest pain by simply telling them to have more faith, or by quoting a Bible verse to them, ironically seems like the least Christ-like approach imaginable.

On this side of heaven, I'm not sure if we'll have perfect answers to these messy questions. I'm not sure where the line intersects between God's sovereign protection and the natural consequences of man's sinful free will. Though theologians have debated these issues for centuries, I'm not sure they've ever discovered a theological truth more profound than the simple promise that God is with us in our pain. He doesn't forsake us in our darkest hour. Psalm 34:18 says, *"The Lord is close to the brokenhearted and saves those who are crushed in spirit."*

Alyssa chose to hold onto that simple promise even on the days when her faith felt fragile. She chose to trust that God is still good even though she was experiencing the worst of human depravity. Eventually her nightmare ended. Her husband, Tyler, and other loved ones helped give her the strength to bring these secrets out into the light and now her former stepfather is behind bars where he belongs. Alyssa and her family are safe. She'll never again have to fear him.

While many others in similar situations like Alyssa's have grown bitter, hard-hearted and faithless as a response to their pain, Alyssa has grown more compassionate, more faithful and more joyful. While many others have chosen to stuff their pain down deep where they never speak of it, Alyssa and her sister Kayla have found the strength to share their testimonies as a way to give help and hope to other survivors of abuse. These strong women and their families are heroes of mine and I'm truly honored to call them friends.

Some people argue that modern-day miracles don't happen anymore. I look at people like Alyssa and see her joy, her healing, her happy marriage and her faith as nothing short of miraculous. It takes a supernatural God and a faith-filled human heart to create the kind of story that Alyssa is now living. Her life is a vivid reminder that God's healing power is bigger than our biggest heartbreak. It's a beautiful glimpse of heaven, where He will wipe every tear from our eyes and make all things new as we experience eternal healing in His presence.

I pray you never have to endure the horrors of Alyssa's childhood, but in whatever you face, know that Jesus is with you in it. Just like the Lord was present in the fiery furnace (Daniel 3), the lion's den (Daniel 6), the imprisonments of the apostles (Acts 5, 12, and 16)—along with the countless other pains and injustices suffered by the forerunners of our faith in the Bible—God is with you in your pain.

Jesus is present with you in your pain, and He loves you. He will carry you through this. He will make it right someday. He is preparing a place for you in heaven where there will be no more pain or injustice. If you'll cling to these truths in your darkest hours, you won't need the strength to survive the pain, but it will be the Lord's strength carrying you through.

Nearly every marriage encounters a dynamic where one or both spouses have faced past trauma. Perhaps the trauma isn't as severe as what Alyssa endured, but regardless of the specifics, all pain from the past can cause more pain in the present if we don't face it in a healthy way. Part of what makes Alyssa and Tyler's story so inspiring is that they chose to face this trauma together. Tyler gave Alyssa strength, compassion and support. Alyssa trusted Tyler by confiding in him and allowing him to be a partner in every aspect of her healing journey.

Tyler and Alyssa have overcome remarkable obstacles to forge a rock-solid, happy and healthy family. They're living proof that it's possible to move forward together through anything if you're willing to get the help you need, trust in God's goodness, and face every issue in partnership with your spouse.

If you're trying to work through any struggle without your spouse or without God, I encourage you to stop trying to do it alone. Don't shut your spouse out. A healthy married couple shares everything—the good things and the hard things—with each other. With God and one another, your marriage can endure any storm and find healing from any wound.

Alyssa's courage to embrace healing has been an inspiration to so many people. Her faith and joy in the aftermath of such brutality gives me hope that Jesus is powerful enough to bring healing to any wound if we'll trust Him. All of us have emotional wounds and scars, and they will either create bitterness within our hearts or tenderness within our hearts depending on how we choose to pursue the healing process.

We know this is a heavy story to share at the start of a chapter on sex, but we believe that it's important to acknowledge the hard truth that past sexual trauma is a reality for many. Not only for the sake of your sex life, but for healing in every aspect of your marriage, your body, your mind and your soul, please talk about these issues and get the help you need. We thank our friends Tyler and Alyssa for their extraordinary courage and for the hope they've given to so many by their willingness to share their story.

Dave

I hope you've never had to deal with past sexual trauma like our friends Alyssa and Tyler, but all of us have some form of sexual baggage. Even if you entered into marriage as a virgin, you had some baggage tied to your mindsets, belief, and experiences related to sex. A lot of my own past baggage came from pornography, which sabotaged my thinking about sex. Much of my current baggage has been related to hormone imbalances related to my thyroid.

I remember the awkward moments of sex education in middle school. I remember it vividly. Every kid in class was blushing and giggling as our teacher tried to keep a straight face, pointing out the various sex organs and what they all do. I remember the charts and the terms. I'll never forget those lessons about words like *penis, vagina, fallopian tubes, ovaries, testicles,* etc. I still giggle a bit even as I type these words out. I suppose we all still have an inner middle schooler inside, no matter how old we get.

For all those biological terms, there was one body part I'm positive was NOT on any of the teacher's pictures or lists: *thyroid.* I had no idea that the thyroid was a sex organ, but apparently it is. In my own experience, I've discovered that a thyroid disorder can start to negatively impact your sex life. My experience isn't unique. Many people struggling with thyroid disorders and auto-immune diseases of all kinds have reported negative side effects in the bedroom.

Sexual side effects are among the most intimate, frustrating and embarrassing of any health issues a person can face. It's relatively easy to say, "My thyroid doesn't work," but it's something else entirely to say, "My penis doesn't work."

As a guy who, alongside my wife, Ashley, coaches thousands of couples worldwide on issues related to marriage and sex—and as a guy who has had a voraciously strong sex drive for most my life—I never thought I'd personally experience any kind of sexual dysfunction. My thyroid condition, with its accompanying plunge in my testosterone levels, changed all that. In addition to an overall drop in energy and mood, I also experienced a precipitous drop in my sex drive and even impediments in my body's ability to perform. Ashley was incredibly encouraging through this. But I was angry, embarrassed, frustrated and at times even horrified. It's a sense of disappointment and powerlessness I wouldn't wish on anybody.

It's vulnerable and personal to write about this experience. But I know so many others are struggling, so I'm sharing this to give you hope. I've actively been working through the mental, physical and hormonal issues impacting our sex life, and I've seen great progress. Briefly, sex was something I actually dreaded because of my anxiety of being able to perform. Now, as it's been for most our marriage, sex is a gift that I always enjoy and look forward to.

Part of what helped us get back to a healthy sex life included simple patience and creating a safe space in our bedroom, where there was never any shame or discouragement. I also actively pursued natural options to help boost my testosterone, including exercise and supplements. I was prescribed hormone therapy by my doctor, but I never actually took it because I was concerned about the side effects. Thankfully, I've been able to bring my testosterone levels back into the normal range through over-the-counter supplements, exercise and overall health.

Whether you're dealing with a medical issue or not, sex is a vital part of a healthy marriage. In the work Ashley and I do at *XO Marriage* and in the weekly episodes on *The Naked Marriage Podcast,* we talk openly and honestly about the keys to a thriving sex life. Here I'm including an excerpt from our book, *The Naked Marriage,* where we list out "The Ten Things Every Married Couple Needs to Know About Sex."

I hope this encourages you and strengthens your marriage inside and outside the bedroom.

Sex is one of the most powerful gifts God ever created. It was designed to bring a man and woman together in a physical, emotional and spiritual bond that would create pleasure, intimacy and also procreation. Marriages that neglect or misuse this gift are headed for frustration and maybe even divorce.

I was reminded of this when some friends of mine were having a marriage crisis and headed for divorce. They had drifted far apart and felt that there was no marriage left. As a last effort, they decided to take a "30-Day Challenge" and committed to having sex every day for a month. By the end of the month, their marriage was stronger and their intimacy was reignited. Their marriage had new momentum which has carried them forward. They're the first to say that "it takes a lot more than sex to build a strong marriage, but it's nearly impossible to build a strong marriage without it!"

Better sex in your marriage requires having the right mindset and establishing the right habits. These ten facts don't represent a comprehensive list, but this is a great start! If you'll apply these ten things in your marriage, I believe your sex life will instantly and dramatically improve!

1. **You should probably be having more of it.**

    Healthy couples make sex a priority. I'm convinced that many (if not most) arguments in marriage stem from sexual frustration. When this aspect of the relationship is neglected, the marriage will start to deteriorate even when other areas of the marriage seem to be going strong. When you make love, you're making your marriage stronger.

2. **Most men see sex as a form of stress relief, BUT most women need stress relief BEFORE they can be in the mindset to make love.**

    There are neurological reasons for these differences, and this is also proof that God has a sense of humor! A husband and wife need to be in tune to one another's needs and desires and self-lessly strive to serve each other. Men and women tend to be wired up differently and each person has his or her own wiring that often supersedes these broader generalizations. Get to know each other. Don't make assumptions. COMMUNICATE and your sex life will improve.

3. **Remember that foreplay is an ALL-DAY EVENT.**

    Foreplay doesn't begin five minutes before you're hoping to get it on. It should begin the moment you wake up in the morning. Every text message, every hug, every act of service, every phone call, every wink, every kiss, every "I love you," and every interaction with each other is an opportunity to make a connection that could culminate in a great climax for you both!

4. Men, if you want to get your wife in the mood, try "Chore-Play." Do the dishes or fold some laundry.

Most men are visual. Seeing their wife in lingerie is enough to instantly get him in the mood. Most women are more complex in their process of becoming aroused. Sure, ladies want their man to look his best, but she also wants her mental to-do list to be clear so she can focus (like we've addressed in #2). Guys, you can help her get in the mindset by doing some household chores. You'll never look hotter in her eyes than when she catches you doing the dishes or folding some laundry!

5. Most people have some sexual "baggage" that they haven't fully discussed with their spouse. Bringing this out into the open could lead to a positive breakthrough in your sex life and in your marriage.

I've interacted with married couples for years, and I've found that there are a lot of sexual secrets spouses keep from each other. Some of these secrets are the result of past abuse and some are the result of past choices. Some of these secrets can also stem from fantasies that one spouse is afraid to say out loud for fear of judgment or rejection. The bottom line is that you need to talk about all of these things with your spouse. Secrecy is the enemy of intimacy. If you want to grow closer to your spouse inside and outside the bedroom, bring your secrets out into the open and encourage him/her to do the same.

6. You should be physically monogamous AND mentally monogamous.

It's sad that we live in a world, where I have to clarify this, but monogamy is the only way a marriage can work. Don't look outside your marriage to fulfill your sexual needs, and I would argue that this includes porn. Bringing another person into your bed or your mind will eventually destroy the intimacy God intended. Sex should be enjoyed exclusively between a husband and a wife. Your sex life starts with your thought life. Keep your thoughts and fantasies focused on your spouse.

7. Better sex starts with getting better in other areas outside the bedroom.

When communication is better, your sex life will usually improve, so talk, text and flirt with each other throughout the day. When you're serving each other's needs in other areas (guys, this means being willing to do the dishes and help more around the house), your sex life will usually improve. When you show genuine thoughtfulness to one another throughout the day, the night is more likely to end well!

8. Don't use sex as leverage.

In some marriages, sex (or denying sex) is used as a way to reward or punish the other spouse. Over time, this practice will cheapen the power of sex, cause resentment and also erode the trust and intimacy in your marriage. Never use sex as a form of leverage, control, reward or punishment. See it as a sacred gift to be freely enjoyed together in marriage.

9. Don't put your sex life on hold while you're raising your kids, or you might end up with an "empty nest" and an "empty marriage"!

When you're raising kids, it takes more time and intentionality to prioritize your sex life, but it's well worth the effort! In fact, I think one of the best gifts you can give your kids is the security that comes from seeing their mom and dad in a loving, affectionate committed relationship with each other. Obviously, still, lock the door while the kids are in the house, but "grossing them out" by kissing and being affectionate with each other is actually a good thing. Have the kind of marriage that makes them actually want to get married someday!

10. Have fun!

Sex is supposed to be fun, so enjoy it! As you do, you'll find your stress levels decreasing, your laughter increasing, and a more positive outlook on life together.

Ashley

Healthy bodies are important for healthy sex, but healthy mindsets are just as important—if not more important. One way that we can sabotage our sex life is by having poor health, but this doesn't just affect our physical bodies. Our poor health can also create insecurities about our own physical appearance.

One of the most common questions we receive on *The Naked Marriage Podcast* and on our social media channels reveals a growing trend in insecurities related to body image and how those insecurities negatively impact a married couple's sex life. We frequently get messages like this:

> *"I want to be at my best for my husband/wife, but I'm so uncomfortable with my own body. I don't even want them looking at me because I feel gross. I feel fat. I have stretch marks. I feel unattractive. I can't compete with the images of 'perfect' people I see all around me. My insecurities are creating sexual frustration and friction in our marriage. What do I do?"*

We all have some level of insecurity. Even those "picture perfect" models we follow on social media and see on television often struggle with body issues. Being in perfect physical shape isn't the solution (although better overall health can be a positive factor). If you want to improve your sex life, but you and/or your spouse have insecurities or body image issues, please consider these three simple principles:

1. Remember what it actually means to have a "naked and unashamed" marriage.

Our first picture of the first married couple in the Bible's Book of Genesis tells us that Adam and Eve were "naked and unashamed." I'm sure they were in good shape, but they weren't "naked and perfect." There were no other humans around to compare themselves to. It wasn't about comparison. It wasn't about looking in the mirror, because mirrors didn't exist.

They had a beautiful connection and a deep intimacy because they were focused on each other's souls, not each other's physical imperfections. Find the courage and vulnerability to be "naked and unashamed." It will take time, but it will create great comfort, security, and intimacy in your marriage bed (and every other part of your marriage, too).

2. If you're uncomfortable making love with the lights on, try candlelight.

I know you might feel uncomfortable being seen, but your spouse wants to see you while you're making love. Most guys are wired up to be more engaged and connected to their wife through visual stimulus. You might not want to see yourself, but he wants to see you! If having all the lights on seems too intimidating, start with candlelight. The soft light is flattering to the figure and it also sets a romantic tone that could make you both feel more comfortable.

3. **Remember that confidence is sexy (and confidence is a choice, not a feeling).**

When we have physical insecurities, it starts a domino effect. You don't feel sexy, so you don't want to think about sex. Then, you get uncomfortable when your spouse initiates sex, so your spouse gets hurt feelings and the marriage gets stuck in a negative cycle of perpetual frustration and miscommunication. If this is accurately describing the current dynamics in your marriage, then you need to change your thinking. It is in your power!

Confidence is not just a feeling. You might not *feel* confident about yourself right now, but you can *choose* to project confidence and before long, you'll actually start feeling it. I'm not making this up! There's plenty of research out there to back this up. According to social psychologist Amy Cuddy's bestselling book and TED talk, *Presence,* even your own posture can affect how you feel about yourself. When you hold your shoulders back and raise your chin up high like a superhero, your mind will shift away from your own insecurities. Isn't that amazing?

We are also affected by what we put on our bodies. Ladies, when was the last time you bought yourself some nice lingerie or sexy sleepwear? If it has been a long time, go treat yourself (and your husband)! Maybe the thought of being in lingerie makes you feel a little insecure and uncomfortable, but I encourage you to get out of your comfort zone and try it. You don't have to spend a lot of money, and it is nice to go to a department store or lingerie shop where someone can help you find what fits you best and makes you feel sexy. You just might be surprised by how confident the nice, new, and well-fitted lingerie or silky sleepwear makes you feel! There's nothing sexier than confidence.

Guys, think about what makes you feel sexy and confident. Treat yourself to some new underwear or clothes that make you feel your best and are something that your wife has told you that she finds sexy. Let it be a surprise, or shop for these items together. Whatever you do, make sure that what you wear to bed (even though it ultimately comes off) is something that brings out your confidence.

There are, of course, many other ways to improve your self-image when it comes to sex beyond the three I listed above, but these three will give you a great start. More than anything, when it comes to sex, remember to talk to your spouse about everything. Healthy sex starts with healthy communication, and you'll discover that communication will also help you improve on other aspects of your marriage as well.

Dave

As we wrap this section about your physical health, I want to leave you with a challenge about commitment and removing all exit strategies that might tempt you to abandon the health of your body, mind, soul, or marriage. One of my favorite examples of removing any exit strategy comes from the prophet Elisha. The Book of 1 Kings in the Old Testament chronicles Elisha's extraordinary story. God called Elisha into a life of ministry, but Elisha wisely understood that embracing his calling would mean letting go of his current career. He had to make a choice between his love for God and his need for the familiarity and financial security of his home.

Elisha was a farmer from a family of farmers. His cattle and his farming equipment represented his family trade, his heritage, and his income. Elisha didn't want the temptation of a comfortable exit strategy in his mind on the days when his new life in ministry might get uncomfortable. Elisha wanted to go all in with God.

To simultaneously celebrate his new calling and publicly display his commitment to God, Elisha threw himself a very unique going-away party. He slaughtered all of his cattle and cooked all their meat by burning all of his farm equipment. He was symbolically and literally lighting fire to his exit strategy.

As he celebrated his new adventure with friends and family that night, they all knew he wouldn't be coming home, because he'd made sure he'd have nothing to come home to. He had removed the temptation. He had eliminated the exit strategy. His love for God moved him to make a dramatic commitment.

God honored Elisha's commitment. Elisha went on to become one of the most significant spiritual leaders in Israel's history. His love, faith, and commitment to God continue to inspire people around the globe.

God wants to do something extraordinary through your life as well. It's going to require commitment. In any quest to improve health, there are going to be many moments when you're tempted to quit—but keep going! Your health is always worth the effort.

In the next chapter, we'll start the final section of the book in which we'll be discussing the most important aspect of your health...the health of your soul. Your mental and physical health last only a lifetime, but the health of your soul has eternal significance. It all begins with building the right foundation.

SECTION THREE:

SOUL

And what do you benefit if you gain the whole world but lose your own soul? Is anything worth more than your soul?

Matthew 16:26 (NLT)

CHAPTER 8:

What's Your Foundation?

Dave

There is no true and lasting health without spiritual health. Our world seems to prioritize the physical and mental aspects of health but leaves out the critical foundation of spiritual health. In Matthew 7:24-27, Jesus tells a story of a wise man who built his house on a solid rock and the foundation helped the house survive the storms of life. There was also a foolish man who built his house on a foundation of sand and the storms toppled his house because it wasn't built on a rock.

Prioritizing spiritual health means building your life and your marriage on the rock. It's giving yourself a secure foundation to weather the storms of life. Storms may be inevitable, but destruction is optional. Faith is what makes all the difference.

As a follower of Christ, I have gained immeasurable hope and peace from trusting in God's Word. In a few pages, I will list a collection of some of the Bible verses that have comforted and strengthened me most on my difficult days. Before I get to them, I want to talk about some specific hope for the difficult days.

Even if you don't yet share my faith, I hope you'll consider this faith-based perspective with an open mind. These tenets of faith have strengthened me and millions of others through our most difficult days and reminded us that we don't have to endure our hardships alone. Jesus has changed my life and He wants to change yours, too.

Faith is the foundation to help your life weather any storm. We all need a solid foundation. Years ago, our kids had an ongoing project of building a fort in the empty lot next to our house. Almost every day after school, they'd meet up with the other neighborhood kids and look for scrap materials to add to their beloved masterpiece. It was really nothing more than some old crates and cardboard stacked together. Every time a storm came, the whole thing fell apart, and they'd have to start the whole process over again.

I wasn't much help on the fort project because I'm terrible with tools. Ashley's dad is a guy who can build and fix anything, so when Ashley married me, she assumed all men had the same skill set. I wish I had those skills, but when I try swinging a hammer, stuff gets broken! Ashley is both the beautiful one and the handy one in our relationship.

The boys wished I had been better at construction, so I could have helped them to build the fort. I did my best to help them gather materials, but my most valuable contribution was a single bit of engineering advice. I told them the fort was going to keep collapsing until they built it securely on a solid foundation. So, they did.

They decided to fasten their fort to a solid foundation of deep roots and big rocks. They worked hard to make sure it didn't budge. When the next storm came, their fort stood strong.

Many marriages resemble that fort. Maybe there's a lot of effort going into building the marriage but it still seems to fall apart. Marriages can crumble because of a lack of effort, but in other cases the marriage fails for the same reasons the boys' fort kept collapsing. It's built with the wrong tools and with no solid foundation.

When Jesus told the story of the wise builder and the foolish builder in Gospel of Matthew, both houses looked the same. The only difference was revealed when a storm came. The strong winds and rains beat against both houses, and the house without a solid foundation collapsed. The house built on the rock stood strong. That's a picture of what building your life on Jesus's teachings can do. Your faith gives you a solid foundation and you will overcome life's storms.

Ashley

As I interact with people who have experienced childhood abuse, marital infidelity, or any form of pain from the past, I've noticed many develop a defense mechanism I call "emotional sunburn." Years ago, our family lived in Florida, and as any Floridian will tell you, you must have sunscreen on hand at all times or you'll get sunburned. I have a fair complexion, and I always make sure to have sunscreen with me when I go to a pool or beach. However, in Florida, I would always end up at a park with our kiddos only to realize that I'd forgotten to bring sunscreen. I'd think it wasn't a big deal at first because we'd only be exposed to the sun for a relatively short time, but then hours later, our unprotected skin would be lobster-red! I'd try to cover the sunburned parts of our skin, but without fail, someone in our family would come give us a slap on the back or a hug that was a little too rough, and we would scream in pain.

Sometimes I'd turn ugly, but we can all get ugly when we're hurting. The person who was touching my sunburned back wasn't trying to hurt me; the pain was from a situation they did nothing to cause. It was a result of my own injury and subsequent hypersensitivity. Still, their touch had inflicted pain, because it exposed a wound that needed healing. Instead of allowing them to rub aloe on me to promote healing, I usually retreated into solitude where I could be grumpy and alone and nobody could hurt me anymore.

In a similar way, I believe many of us have sunburn all over our hearts from being burned in our past. These past wounds, if left untreated, can cause us to overreact in unhealthy ways to our loved ones, pushing others away in an attempt to protect ourselves. Sometimes we even fall into a cycle of inflicting wounds on ourselves to push others away or to feel a sense of control when our lives or relationships feel out of control.

Working with youth as a former middle school teacher and youth ministry leader, I've seen the tragic cycle of self-inflicted pain in the form of eating disorders or cutting, in which young people (usually adolescent girls) will literally cut themselves with a blade. Many psychologists believe these actions are an attempt to regain control when their relationships at home or school have become dysfunctional and out of control. It's a harmful cycle that creates more pain instead of healing.

These kinds of behaviors aren't a new phenomenon. In fact, the expression "cutting off your nose to spite your face" originates from a historical account of a medieval nun who famously encouraged self-mutilation as a means of self-preservation. Ebba the Younger was a ninth-century nun at a convent in Europe during a time when Vikings from the north were pillaging the land. A group of these Vikings were attempting to break into Ebba's convent one night, so she decided to take drastic action to protect her chastity from what she believed was an imminent sexual assault.

She went to the kitchen, found a knife, and went to work sawing off her nose and her upper lip, leaving a bloody, grotesque sight. She encouraged all the other women to follow her example. Each nun took a knife and performed this painful act of self-mutilation. When the Vikings finally broke through the outer doors and found the nuns, the men were so horrified by the sight that they burned down the convent, killing all the women inside. It was a terrible tragedy.

I recognize that this story is probably more of an interesting anecdote from history than a practical lesson in modern relationships. I doubt you've ever been so brokenhearted or afraid that sawing off your nose and upper lip seemed like the best possible course of action! Still, I believe this paints a vivid picture of the drastic measures people are capable of taking to protect themselves from potential pain or heartbreak—even when they harm themselves in the process.

Sometimes we can subconsciously do things to make ourselves seem ugly or intimidating to drive people away, because we're afraid if we allow others close to us, we'll only be hurt again. This kind of behavior might give us the illusion of power and safety that comes from isolation, but it will also hold us captive in a prison of solitude where we never experience true love.

Whatever you may have done or whatever may have been done to wound you in the past, healing is possible. God wants you to live a life of love. He wants you to experience rich, meaningful relationships—especially when it comes to your relationship with Him, your spouse, and even yourself. He wants to bring you to a place of healing so you can experience life and love in all of its fullness. However, we live in a society that applauds independence and the notion of achieving success all by ourselves.

We are often groomed to do whatever it takes to protect ourselves because "no one else will." Being independent and self-sufficient is certainly not a bad thing in and of itself, but it can lead to a lonely existence when we pursue it above all else (and many times we do). In a world where half of marriages end in divorce, we are taught to have one foot in the door and one foot out the door, just to be ready in case our marriage fails. Some individuals even have prenups, secret bank accounts, or money stashes in preparation for the day they may decide to divorce their spouse. What is the common denominator in all of these things? It is the belief that we don't *need* each other...that we can and should live our lives as if we were never married. This is a big lie that sends husbands and wives into a lonely marital existence for years, and some even decide to call it quits.

So, what does a lonely marriage look like? It is two married people living very disconnected lives. Each spouse is highly engaged in his or her work during the day and doesn't choose to involve his or her spouse in the workplace functions. There are no sweet texts or phone calls to connect with each other during the day. When they get home at night, both spouses are hyper-focused on finishing up their work, getting with their friends, and/or tending to the kids and all of their needs.

All conversation seems to center around what has been done or what needs to be done to take care of the kids, home, and finances. Both the husband and wife are much more concerned with setting up "Girls Night Out" or "Night Out with the Guys" than a date night. They rarely have sex, and when they do, there is a lack of connection. They both seem to be civil with each other, especially in public places, but there is frustration in the under-current of all of their communication.

They both feel stifled by the other and even resent most of what their spouse does. The husband and wife try to find reasons to not spend time together because the time they spend together is the loneliest and most exhausting part of their day. Both have completely lost sight of what brought them together in the first place. Somewhere along the way they lost their togetherness in an effort to pursue their independence. After all, they have each been doing their "own thing" and handling it all just fine, so they don't really need each other, do they? Of course, they do!

If this scenario describes your marriage, please know that it doesn't have to be this way. You can have the close, intimate marriage that you so desire. Here are some steps you can take to turn things around:

1. You need to engage in meaningful conversation with your spouse every day.

If you find that you are in a lonely marriage, there has been a breakdown of communication somewhere along the way. You need to start communicating again. These conversations involve more than, "Kids have soccer on Friday" or "Office party is on Saturday night" or "What's for dinner?" Laugh together and talk about your hopes, fears, and dreams. You both need to reconnect, and conversation is the bridge that will get you there.

I also encourage you to start praying together every night. Your first prayer may be just asking God to help you get out of this lonely time in your marriage, but then you can add to your prayer list together. Remember: your individual and collective soul health is imperative to cultivating a healthy, lasting, and fulfilling marriage.

2. We must remove anything that is perpetrating the loneliness in our marriage.

Are you spending more time with your friends than your spouse? If so, you need to spend less time with those friends and more time with your spouse. Invest in your friendship with your spouse! Are you staying at work too late? If so, you need to rearrange your work schedule so you can spend more time at home. Start connecting with your spouse throughout the day. This can be as simple as a sweet or flirtatious text that says, "I love you and hope you are having a great day" or a quick phone call to check in. This lets your partner know that you care. You will also feel cared for when your spouse makes you a high priority and not an afterthought.

3. **Be sure that your tone, body language, words, and actions towards your spouse are loving, respectful, and inclusive.**

Sometimes, you can make your spouse feel all alone just by the negative tone of your voice and careless body language, and you may not even realize that you are doing it. Be sure to pay close attention to how you respond to one another. Do you smile when your spouse walks in the room, or do you greet him or her? Do you speak kindly to your spouse, whether in person or around others? Do you take time each day to do something kind and thoughtful for your spouse?

If you can answer "yes" to all of these, then you are on the right track. If not, there is room for improvement, and you can take those steps toward improvement today. Don't wait! Show your spouse how much you care. Lean in and engage with them. Don't settle for a lonely marriage. Over time, you will see what a difference these steps will make, and you both will cultivate a thriving marriage.

4. **You both must understand and admit that you need each other.**

Some of you may think that needing your spouse shows weakness, makes you "needy," or gives them too much power over your life. But the honest truth is a marriage will quickly become a lonely place unless both spouses are willing to lean on each other and care for one another as God intended. You are not giving up your individuality; you are trading your completely independent lives for a supportive, *interdependent* union with your spouse.

Please understand that I am not encouraging or promoting an unhealthy co-dependent marriage in which spouses emotionally abuse each other and neediness runs rampant. A healthy, balanced marriage is like a beautiful ballroom dance where the husband and wife are completely intertwined and in tune to one another, with God leading them in their journey together. He gave us such a gift when He gave us our spouse. He never meant for us to live in a lonely marriage—or a lonely existence, period—so let's embrace and cherish the beautiful gift of our marriage. Let your love and faith in the Lord defeat the loneliness.

> *Consequently, you are no longer foreigners and strangers, but fellow citizens with God's people and also members of his household, built on the foundation of the apostles and prophets, with Christ Jesus himself as the chief cornerstone. In him the whole building is joined together and rises to become a holy temple in the Lord. And in him you too are being built together to become a dwelling in which God lives by his Spirit.* (Ephesians 2:19-22)

Dave

There's a show on TV called *Hoarders*. It's about people who just accumulate junk and never get rid of it. Their homes are filled with piles of trash so high that the only creatures who can navigate the house are roaches and rats. My dorm rooms used to look a little bit like that. The show is both sad and disgusting, but on a spiritual level, I think a lot of us live our lives as hoarders.

We don't mean to become hoarders; it just naturally happens over time until one day, we're buried under a pile of junk. We've got to be willing to clear away negative things that are taking up space, to make room for new things that will bring peace back into our lives. Once we make these choices, we'll be in a position to help others find healing as well.

In Colossians 3, the Bible paints a picture of some of the junk that's taking up too much space in our minds, hearts, and lives: *"But now is the time to get rid of anger, rage, malicious behavior, slander, and dirty language"* (Colossians 3:8 NLT).

We can't get rid of this kind of junk by throwing it in a garbage bag. We need to pray for God to remove it and be willing to drastically change our attitudes, behaviors, and decisions to push the remnants of these negative things out of our lives. Once they start to clear away, it's time to bring in new things to replace them. Just a few verses later, the Bible tells us what those new things should be: *"Since God chose you to be the holy people he loves, you must clothe yourselves with tenderhearted mercy, kindness, humility, gentleness, and patience"* (Colossians 3:12 NLT).

These aren't things we can pick up at the mall. Again, we have to ask God to fill our lives with these attributes and be diligent in our efforts to hold onto them. We must allow God's Word to renew our minds and give us a new way of thinking that leads to a new way of living. He wants to bring you healing. Trust him enough to let go of those things that are holding you back. Those are toxic forces sabotaging your marriage. Once you have the faith to let go of the junk, your hands and your heart will be open to receive healing.

Keep in mind that this is not a one-time process. Negative clutter has a tendency to keep working its way into our lives, so this should become a lifestyle pattern of clearing out the old (negative stuff) and making room for the new (positive stuff). Don't let yourself get buried by negativity. Let love sweep through your life and replace that junk with joy.

This process begins by building your marriage and your life on the right foundation. Make the commitment that, from this time forward, you're going to follow God's plan for your marriage and build your home on the foundation of His Word. Remember: storms in marriage are inevitable, but destruction is optional. Having the right foundation is what makes all the difference, and the health of your soul will be the difference-maker when you face hardships in life.

With or without faith, tough days are going to come our way, but faith makes those tough days lose their power over us.

One of the most difficult (and important) ways to improve the health of your soul is to let go of the toxic force of unforgiveness. Have you ever experienced a betrayal in your own life, or witnessed a travesty in the life of someone else, and thought to yourself, "I can forgive up to a certain point, but I could never forgive something like that!" There's a sense of justice within us that can be offended by grace. After all, when someone wrongs us, they should be punished, right?

These are important questions, and they're far too important to answer with mere opinion. We need to look straight to God's Word, because God is not only the Creator of love, He's also the Creator of grace. One of the longest narratives recorded in the Bible is found in the book of Genesis. There we're introduced to a character named Jacob, who had twelve sons. Jacob's name was eventually changed to "Israel," and his sons became the patriarchs of the twelve tribes of Israel.

Jacob was a hero of the faith, but he was far from perfect. His polygamist lifestyle and his dysfunctional approach to parenting created insecurity and unhealthy competition among his sons. Eventually, Joseph emerged as a favorite of his father. Jacob would give special gifts and recognitions to Joseph, and the brothers hated Joseph for it.

One day, Joseph was telling his brothers about a dream he'd had in which they were all bowing down to him. It proved to be the breaking point for the jealous siblings. They threw Joseph down into an abandoned well and started plotting the best way to make him disappear permanently.

Several of the brothers wanted to kill him, but then decided they may as well profit from him instead. A band of foreigners were traveling past on their way to Egypt, so the brothers hoisted Joseph out of the well and sold him to the foreigners. They covered up their crime by putting animal blood all over Joseph's coat and bringing it home to their father.

Joseph was sold into slavery by his own brothers! I don't know what kind of heartbreak you've experienced in your life, but I doubt many of us have experienced that level of betrayal. The heartbreaking grief nearly killed Jacob. He pledged to mourn the loss of his son for the rest of his life.

At the age of seventeen years old, Joseph was placed on an auction block and sold to an Egyptian official named Potiphar. The young slave was taken to his new home in shackles. His dreams were shattered. His life would never be the same.

Joseph could have allowed bitterness and resentment to take root in his heart. He could have replayed his brothers' crime over and over in his mind. He could have given up and ended his own life. But he didn't do any of those things. Instead, he chose to trust God and make the most of his situation.

Joseph started working hard and earning his master's trust. It wasn't long before Joseph was placed in charge of the entire estate.

His work ethic had earned the respect of everyone in the house. Life was going as well as it could go for a young man with no freedom.

But Joseph's story was about to take a dramatic twist. Potiphar's wife took notice of the handsome young slave, and she began trying to seduce him. Joseph could have justified giving in to her advances and satisfying his own natural drives, but he refused to dishonor his God or his earthly master in such a way. He repeatedly refused to give in to the temptation.

She gradually grew furious at his repeated rejections and decided to punish him for it. She told her husband that Joseph had tried to rape her, and Joseph was thrown into a dungeon as a result.

At this point, I think most of us would have completely given up hope. We may have lost all faith in God's goodness. Joseph could have said, "God, if you're out there, you obviously don't care about me. I've done everything I can do to live my life with honor and faith, and I've been betrayed over and over. I've gone from being a free man to a slave and now a prisoner. It's all my brothers' fault. I'll never forgive them for ruining my life!"

Joseph didn't take that approach. Instead, he decided to trust God as best he could from within the prison walls. He assumed that if God was allowing him to be in this prison, it must be for a good reason, as part of a bigger plan. Joseph kept his faith. He refused to allow bitterness to take root in his heart. He refused to hate his brothers or his accusers or anyone else.

It wasn't long before Joseph had won the warden's respect and was given freedom to run the entire prison under the warden's supervision. Joseph made the most of a bad situation. He also used his unique, God-given ability to interpret dreams. He deciphered the hidden messages God communicated to the other inmates while they slept. Joseph's unshakable faith in God changed the culture of the prison and encouraged men who had lost all hope.

After seven years as a slave and seven more years as a prisoner, Joseph received a life-changing opportunity. The pharaoh, the sovereign leader of Egypt, was being tormented by dreams no one could interpret. Joseph's reputation had grown beyond the prison walls, and Pharaoh called on the prisoner to make sense of his dreams.

Joseph told Pharaoh that God was telling him what was about to happen in Egypt. A period of great abundance would soon come to Egypt, followed by a period of severe famine. If preparations weren't made and food wasn't systematically stored during the good years, Egypt would starve during the famine.

Pharaoh saw the wisdom and confidence in the young prisoner before him and appointed him governor over all of Egypt. Joseph would be in charge of the empire, as second-in-command to Pharaoh.

That's quite a turn of events! Joseph was promoted from the bottom rung on the social ladder to the very top within a matter of minutes, a God-given opportunity made possible because of Joseph's faithfulness during the difficult years. Our response to present difficulties will often determine our level of future opportunities.

Let's fast-forward to the famine. Joseph was ruling well and had earned the respect of a grateful nation. Not only did Egypt have enough stored food for the Egyptians, but foreigners were traveling from different lands to purchase food. In a moment of poetic justice, Joseph's brothers ended up standing before him, hoping to buy food and bowing at his feet. It was the image he had dreamed would happen decades earlier.

His brothers didn't recognize him. They were convinced he was dead, and they had lived with unspeakable guilt all the years since betraying him. Joseph put his brothers through a series of tests to measure their current level of integrity, and when he couldn't wait any longer, he revealed himself.

Joseph was overcome with emotion, and his brothers were overcome with terror. They believed they were about to face divine retribution and execution for their terrible crime. What they experienced instead was unmerited, radical grace. At the end of this ordeal, Joseph spoke some of the most profound and grace-filled words recorded in the Bible:

> But Joseph replied, "Don't be afraid of me. Am I God, that I can punish you? You intended to harm me, but God intended it all for good. He brought me to this position so I could save the lives of many people. No, don't be afraid. I will continue to take care of you and your children." So, he reassured them by speaking kindly to them. (Genesis 50:19–21 NLT)

Joseph forgave his brothers. Not only did he forgive them, but he encouraged them so that they would not continue to punish themselves for what they had done to him so many years ago. They had meant it all for evil, but God had been working in this plan all along and meant it all for good. He used the ordeal to teach them all lessons of grace and the faithfulness of God.

Had Joseph executed his brothers, the nation of Israel would have died before it even began. Instead, a family was reborn, and a nation was established—all because of grace. Love won. You will win too when you choose to forgive. Forgiveness is choosing to release a prisoner only to find out the prisoner was you. Embrace grace. It's the first step to a free and healthy soul.

Ashley

The story of Joseph is an ancient one of extending radical grace, but there are also modern-day stories of radical grace happening in our midst. One of these examples happened after the death of our friend, Derek Elam. Derek was a friend of Dave's, but also a friend of mine whom I'd known for years before Dave and I ever met. Derek was the kind of person who could easily befriend people of all ages. It was rare for him to meet someone he didn't like or someone who didn't like him. He seemed to have no enemies.

In 2004, Derek was young, strong, smart, talented, ambitious, and ready to take on the world. He was preparing to move from our hometown of Georgetown, Kentucky, to Nashville, Tennessee. Nashville might not seem like a huge city for you, but for people from our neck of the woods, moving to Nashville was the equivalent of moving to New York City or Los Angeles. We were all excited for him—and a little jealous at the same time.

On Friday, July 2, Derek was only a few weeks away from his twenty-third birthday and his planned move. He had scheduled to be off work so he could hang out with family and friends, but he decided at the last minute to pick up a few more shifts at the music store where he worked near the University of Kentucky's campus. He wanted to make some last-minute cash to take to Tennessee.

He was manning the cash register on a quiet Tuesday afternoon, selling records and CDs (which, for you younger readers, is what we listened to in the old days before iTunes was invented). I'm sure he was enjoying the day the way he seemed to always enjoy life. He had no way of knowing that he was about to come face-to-face with the most dangerous enemy he would ever encounter.

A man burst through the door and put a gun in Derek's face. He demanded all the money in the cash register. Derek immediately emptied the cash register and held his hands in the air, but the thief still put the .22-caliber gun to Derek's head and pulled the trigger. With our friend lying on the floor in a pool of his own blood, the gunman fled with the cash. It was less than one hundred dollars.

When we received the heartbreaking call, Dave and I rushed to the hospital as fast as we could. We walked into that emotionally charged ICU waiting room to see Derek's family and many friends crying, hoping, and praying for a miracle.

We made our way through the maze of chaos and found the room where he was on life-support. I'll never forget that crushing feeling of seeing a friend who had been so full of life now lying lifeless in a hospital bed, hooked up to machines. It didn't seem real. It didn't seem possible. And yet, it had happened, and there was no way to undo it. Derek died that night. This story would be unimaginably tragic if this were the end of the story, but because of what Jesus has done on our behalf, death is never the end of the story!

Derek's mom, Diana, had always had a strong faith, but we never really know how strong our faith is until it's tested by tragedy. Here in the midst of the worst tragedy a parent could ever experience, she exuded a peace that couldn't be explained apart from God. Through her tears, she comforted others. She smiled as she talked about how Derek was now with Jesus. She reassured us all that death wasn't the end of this story, and we would see him again.

She carried that same attitude into the funeral. She chose to wear white instead of the traditional black. She said that while it was a heartbreaking day for her and for all of us who cared about Derek, it was a glorious day for him, because he was now home in heaven where there's no more pain or sickness or crime or death. With a broken heart, she found the strength to give thanks to God in her darkest hour.

For most of us, the grieving process was a combination of sadness and anger. We felt sadness over the unspeakable loss and anger due to the senseless act of violence that caused it. We all wanted justice, and we wanted it fast. The city rallied together, and a manhunt ensued for Derek's killer.

It wasn't long before the perpetrator was apprehended. He was a young man about Derek's age. He was a repeat offender who had committed murder on two separate occasions, and had recently been released on parole for a murder he had committed as a juvenile.

As much temptation and justification as there might have been for hatred towards this man, Derek's mom chose a different path. She wisely realized that bitterness doesn't exist in a vacuum. When we harbor a grudge toward someone, it doesn't stay isolated to the person who wronged us. It poisons us, spills over, and eventually harms our friends and family as well.

Bitterness spreads rapidly, but thankfully, so does love. Diana refused to have a bitter heart. Of course, she wanted justice for her son, but hatred has nothing to do with justice. She refused to hate the man who murdered Derek. She chose instead to respond with love.

She prayed for this man. She prayed for his conviction, but she also prayed for his salvation. She prayed that God would give her the strength to not only forgive him but to love him. In a supernatural way, God granted her prayer and changed her heart. She no longer saw the man as a monster. She saw him as a lost and wounded child who desperately needed the love and grace of his heavenly Father.

Ultimately, the courts did their job, and justice was carried out. The man was convicted and sentenced to life in prison, but Diana's faith and love continues to extend to the gunman who killed her son. Her faith has inspired many. Below is her summation of all that's happened in her own words:

> "I continue to pray he (Derek's murderer) will come to know Jesus and ask God to let me know when that happens. I had a dream one night shortly after this happened that he and Derek were in heaven together and he apologized to Derek. Derek said, 'You're here in heaven. That's what matters.' I knew that was God's way of saying this will come to pass. I forgave him the minute I knew of this murder but also believe he should serve out his life in prison. Without Christ, he's a dead man walking no matter where he is. With Christ, he's free no matter where he is. Because I gave this over to God and let him handle it all, I was free of bitterness, anger, unforgiveness, and grudges, which are the fruit of our enemy. Instead God gave me the ability to walk in his fruit of love, joy, peace, patience, kindness, gentleness, faithfulness, and self-control. I am free indeed thanks to our wonderful heavenly Father."

Most of us will probably never encounter the kind of enemy who will threaten our lives or the lives of our children, but there will still be people who hurt you. When you experience the sting of betrayal or rejection, human nature will tempt you to retaliate with revenge, but God has a different and better path for you. When we choose to trust him with the justice part, we can focus on promoting healing and love.

Dave

As we prepare to wrap up this chapter, I want to share a list of the seven most common mistakes our culture perpetuates which sabotage our spiritual health. We are all prone to these mistakes and misaligned priorities. I encourage you to read through this list prayerfully, asking the Holy Spirit to reveal any area where you might currently have "blind spots" or be off course. Also, read through this list with your spouse, asking them to point out areas in your life in need of repair and improvement.

In no particular order, here are the seven most common mistakes we make which sabotage our own spiritual health:

1. We prioritize career and/or hobbies ahead of our family.

Most people tend to be drawn to places that "make sense." In other words, we like our world to have clear rules, roles, and rewards for our actions. In family life, it gets more complicated. We don't always know if we're measuring up. We don't always know what our role should be. It doesn't always "make sense." Because of this, many men and women make the tragic mistake of retreating into their hobbies or careers, trading quality time with family for other pleasures or pursuits. In the end, your family will be all that matters to you. Please don't wait until then to discover this truth. Give them the place of priority they need and deserve in your schedule. They don't need you to be perfect, but they desperately need you to be present!

2. We value our pleasure ahead of our purpose.

As a culture, we have started valuing porn more than true intimacy, sex more than commitment, and "playing the field" more than marriage. We're undisciplined in our finances. We're sloppy. We don't want to delay our gratification. We don't want to pursue anything that might cost us something. This daily temptation has the potential to rob us of our very purpose. We need to ask ourselves, "What do I want my life and my legacy to be about?

Do I want to only live for the moment, or do I want to make an investment with this moment that will outlive me? Do I want temporary pleasure, or do I want a permanent, positive impact?" Ask those questions, answer them honestly, and be willing to adjust accordingly.

3. We value those who agree with us but "write off" those who don't.

We used to live in a society where we could have civil discourse around issues that mattered. Now, whenever someone disagrees with our position, we attack with spiteful vengeance, reducing their argument to an internet meme and diminishing their dignity by calling them names or "unfriending" them on social media. We are far too quick to label people or put them in boxes. When we refuse to have respectful dialogue around our different convictions and beliefs, we give away a piece of our own humanity, we destroy relationships, and we miss out on the opportunity to learn from those who don't think or feel exactly like we do. One of the truest tests of mature manhood and womanhood is the ability to disagree with someone while still remaining respectful.

4. We care more about "getting credit" than having character.

In our success-obsessed culture, we have lost sight of the value of true integrity. Character is measured by what we do when nobody is watching, but these days it seems as if we don't value *anything* if nobody is watching. We think we can have a closet full of dirty secrets as long as we protect our reputations. We've taken on a shallow and selfish mindset deserving of the condemnation Jesus gave the Pharisees when he said they were *"whitewashed tombs—beautiful on the outside but filled on the inside with dead people's bones"* (Matthew 23:27 NLT). We need to start valuing integrity over income, character over charisma, and reality over reputation.

5.   **We elevate our own agenda above everyone else's.**

While there's something to be said for having a sense of personal responsibility and work ethic, many of us have taken this too far. We have such a need for control that we push everyone away—including God—if they get in the way of our own agendas. Our need for control creates unnecessary stress, inflated egos, or both. We need to be humble enough to know that there's a God, and we're not Him. I doubt Drake was rapping about a biblical worldview when he wrote his hit song, "God's Plan," but I hope it reminds listeners that God's plan needs to be the centerpiece of your life and dreams. We need to trust God's plan instead of always forcing our own.

6.   **We put ourselves ahead of our spouse and set the wrong example for our children.**

One of the main reasons why dating relationships are so broken is that the examples from so many husband-wife relationships are broken. Many men and women have redefined what marriage should be using selfish criteria. We often use our spouses to fulfill our own needs, or make selfish demands of them instead of truly loving them. Your spouse deserves better. Our kids deserve better. If your marriage is struggling and you don't know where to start, please check out the many marriage articles, videos, events, and resources we have available at XOMarriage.com.

7.   **We value "networking" over genuine friendships.**

In our quest for personal and professional achievement, we've tended to see other people as commodities and assets instead of friends. In the process, we've lost sight of what friendship really means. We find ourselves surrounded by people who owe us favors, but we don't know what it means to do something kind for someone with no thought of repayment. We need to get back to basics. We need to invest in meaningful friendships. Relationships are what give meaning to life. When you and I are on our deathbeds someday, our faith, our families, and our friends will be all that matters.

There are, of course, more mistakes than just these seven, but I believe these are the most common ones. If you'll watch out for these, you'll be protecting yourself and your marriage from some common and dangerous missteps. In the next chapter, we'll continue the conversation about the health of your soul by exploring how to find spiritual healing from the wounds and baggage we all carry.

CHAPTER 9:

Spiritual Healing

Ashley

Spiritual healing begins the moment you realize that you are truly, fully and unconditionally loved. One of my favorite stories in the Bible is about a young woman who discovered her identity through Jesus eyes, and it changed everything. If we look closely, I believe all of us can find parallels in our own stories, too. It's a powerful story of spiritual healing that we find in Luke 7:36-50.

This young woman was infamous in her town because of her profession. She was the subject of whispers, gossip, scorn, disgrace, and judgment. Many of her clients would gladly employ her services in the cover of darkness and then point hypocritical, self-righteous fists in her direction in the daylight.

She had no place in society. She had no respect from her community, and she had no self-respect either. She felt she had no escape. She thought she deserved every harsh word and judgmental glare she had ever received. She believed this was simply who she was and all she could ever hope to be. She was a prostitute.

This woman had heard that Jesus would be visiting the home of a prominent religious leader in the community that day. She'd already heard Jesus's words and experienced His compassion. She was one of the many who had been changed by His love. He was perhaps the first man in her life who had looked at her with neither lust nor judgment in His eyes. Only love. Only compassion. He never touched her body, but He had been the first to touch her heart.

His love had broken her and invigorated her at the same time. She was a woman who had known the embrace of many men, but she had never known real love until she found Jesus—or rather, until Jesus found her. It was the purest and most powerful force she had ever experienced. His words made her see herself in a completely different light.

At first, she wasn't sure how to respond to His love. All the confusion and past hurt left so many chaotic cracks in her heart that she struggled to believe she was even capable of giving or receiving love. Even still, she was drawn to Jesus with a force beyond anything she could explain. His love had given her things she'd never experienced before: healing for her past and hope for her future.

The tumultuous tug-of-war in her mind and heart eventually led her to a crossroads between her old life of sin and a new life made possible by the love of Jesus. She knew that the decisions she made next about which path to pursue would define her present and her future. I'm sure she was tempted to retreat to familiar ground, which would have meant the comfortable misery of her old life. However, for the first time, she dared to dream of a new life—and maybe even a new identity. Jesus love had made it possible, and if she didn't respond to His love immediately, she feared she would regret it for eternity. Now was the time to act.

Before she could talk herself out of it, she found herself wandering into unfamiliar territory. She was an uninvited guest at a religious leader's home. Based on the customs and laws of the day, she could have been dragged out into the street immediately and killed by stoning, but her love for Jesus was a stronger force than her instinct for self-preservation.

She made her way to Jesus as the party atmosphere of the room grew quiet at the scandalous scene unfolding before them. She knelt at the feet of Jesus—feet that would soon be nailed to a cross to pay the price for her sins and ours as well—and she began to anoint them with expensive perfume. This alabaster jar filled with perfume was perhaps her only valuable possession. She poured it over the feet of her Savior.

The thick aroma quickly overwhelmed the room. The contents of the jar represented her old life. For her, the fragrance was the aroma of freedom. It was as if she were pouring out her very heart and soul.

The perfume was so valuable that it would have been a form of currency—a savings account, of sorts, of her earnings. It also represented her future in the seduction business, as a few drops of that fragrance would have made her more appealing to potential clients on the streets.

None of that mattered now. She was pouring out her past, her present, and her future onto the feet of Jesus. In a scene of reckless abandon and uncontrolled emotion, the woman began to weep. As her tears mixed with the perfume, she kissed the feet of Jesus and dried them with her hair.

The host of the party, however, didn't see this as a beautiful act of love, but rather as an awkward interruption of his meal. The man began to mentally judge this woman *and* Jesus for allowing such a scene. Knowing the man's thoughts, Jesus took the opportunity to set the self-righteous host straight.

For all in the room to hear and for those reading about this woman in the Bible for generations to come, Jesus applauded the young woman's unabashed act of love. His affirmation gave her the courage and strength she needed to move forward with her new life.

She experienced true peace, and it was all made possible because of the Prince of Peace. Jesus even proclaimed that, for all time, wherever the good news of the Bible is taught, this woman's act of love would be remembered and discussed. True to His words, her example has been a model of love, courage, and faith that has inspired billions over the last two thousand years. Her inclusion in this book is just another footnote in her enduring legacy.

Anytime we love someone, we will eventually be compelled to make a selfless sacrifice. Jesus didn't need this woman's perfume, but she needed to give it. The very act of the sacrifice became an important milestone in her journey.

Sometimes love will compel us to sacrifice because of the need in our own hearts, and other times we'll be called to sacrifice to meet a tangible need for the ones we love.

In some situations, the sacrifice will become an ongoing aspect of the relationship. We see this every day in people working to provide for their children, caring for aging parents, or even caring for their own spouses. Those selfless, sacrificial acts are beautiful and powerful expressions of love. They courageously pave a path to spiritual healing, which blesses both the one who is healed and the one who is helping.

Dave

My Great Uncle Joe has dedicated his life to helping others find spiritual healing through a relationship with Jesus Christ. It was this lifelong calling that prompted him to get out of his bed at midnight almost forty years ago. He leaned over to his wife and told her that he had to go do something. He felt strongly that God had given him an important assignment, and it couldn't wait until morning. It seemed like a crazy mission, but he knew in his gut that it had to be done right away.

She was way too tired to argue or ask many questions, so he kissed her on the forehead, put on a jacket over his pajamas, and walked out to his truck. He drove to the outskirts of their little Indiana farm town and pulled into the parking lot of a place he'd driven past a thousand times but had never gone inside. The sign read, "Welcome to the Red Fox Bar."

The Red Fox was infamous for the brawlers, strippers, and scoundrels who frequented the place. The man who owned and tended the bar was a legendary wild man named Jughead. His real name was Leon, but everyone called him Jughead, or Jug for short. No one seemed sure where or how the nickname had originated, but it seemed to fit him well.

Jug looked up from the bar and saw my uncle Joe walking in wearing his PJs and house slippers. Uncle Joe was a preacher and never had much use for alcohol, so the bartender had to do a double take to be sure of what he was seeing. He finally shook his head and laughed out loud. "Well, I never! What are you doing in here, preacher man? What can I pour you to drink?"

"Hey, Jug," Uncle Joe replied with a yawn. "I'm not here for a drink."

"Well, you do realize it's a bar, don't you? If you're not here for a drink, then what on earth are you here for?"

Uncle Joe walked up to the bar and said, "This has never happened to me before, but I believe God woke me up tonight and gave me a very specific assignment. He wanted me to drive down here and give you a message."

Jug exploded with laughter and smacked the bar with amused delight. "Oh, God has a message for me, does he? I'll bet he does!

You Christians are always telling me about God's message for me. What is it this time? Are you here to tell me that I'm going to hell for running a bar or that my wife's going to hell because she used to be a stripper? Does God want me to know that I'm worthless? I heard that message my entire childhood from my dad, so I certainly don't need to hear it again. So, tell me, preacher, what is God's message for me?"

Uncle Joe put his hands down on the bar and looked Jug in the eyes. With a piercing conviction and compassion in his voice, he said, "Jug, God wanted me to tell you that he loves you and he has an extraordinary plan for your life."

Jug immediately looked down at the bar and began wiping it off with a towel as if Uncle Joe was invisible. Joe turned to walk back outside, thinking his assignment was complete and he could go back to bed, but before he got to the exit, he heard Jug's voice.

"Wait!"

Uncle Joe turned around, and Jug was standing behind the bar with tears streaming down his face. With a quiver in his voice, he asked, "Is that true? Does God really love me? Nobody has ever told me that before."

Uncle Joe walked back to the bar and sat down. The two men talked and laughed and cried until the early hours of the morning. Jug prayed the first prayer of his life at that bar, and he asked God to forgive him of his sins. Jug committed to living the rest of his life following Jesus, embracing God's limitless love, and sharing that love with others. Right there at the bar that night, love changed Jug's life forever.

Jug put a "For Sale" sign out in front of the Red Fox and refused to sell the building to anyone who would continue using it as a bar. He walked away from his old life and wholeheartedly embraced a new one. His personal transformation caused such a stir in the small town that a revival broke out, beginning with his wife (the retired stripper) and many of the patrons of the bar. Jug eventually became a preacher, and today he continues to live out his promise of living a life of love and grace and helping others to do the same.

I love this story, because it's a reminder of the infinite power of love. Once people realize that they're truly, fully, unconditionally loved, it changes everything. Maybe you've forgotten. Or maybe, like Jug, you've never been told in the first place. But God loves you and he has an extraordinary plan for your life. Spiritual healing begins once you allow that truth to penetrate into your heart and soul.

Ashley

I absolutely love how that story is a real-life example of a Christ-follower being obedient to the Lord and getting out of his comfort zone to tell others how much Jesus loves them—even when it's inconvenient and doesn't make complete sense to him at the time. The truth is, following Jesus can be a messy process, much like the woman who poured out perfume on Jesus's feet and dried her ever-flowing tears with her hair.

Recently, I read a book by John Hambrick called *Move Toward the Mess*, in which he reminds us that we are most like Jesus when we choose to pursue and promote spiritual healing in our lives, and the lives of others, by embracing the messy parts of our world. Jesus consistently embraced the messiest people and parts of society. He wasn't afraid of how things looked or what others might think of Him. Jesus moved toward the mess with a kind of love and grace that completely changed minds, hearts, and lives forever. He continues to do this today.

As Christians, we sometimes put ourselves inside a box. We stick with other like-minded Christians and do our best to protect ourselves and our families from "those other people" who don't think like us, or do things like us, or even look like us. We might send them food or packages. We might even donate clothes to them and feel like we've done our part. But is that what Jesus would do? Hambrick doesn't think so, and near the middle of his book, he shares one story in particular that has helped me to think outside of the box when it comes to reaching the lost.

Hambrick shares the story of a young couple who lived in an area of town that most considered the "sketchy section" to be avoided at all costs. Even so, this couple decided to embrace their new community—including the junkies and prostitutes lining the streets. They noticed that many of these men and women were wandering around and in need of food, so they, along with another young couple, decided to set up a hot dog stand every Sunday at 5. They gave away all the hot dogs for free until they were gone. The news got out, and soon they had a large crowd of regulars every time they set up the stand.

Over time, the couple got to know one prostitute on a more personal level. Their hearts broke as they listened to her share the details of her past. Tragically, it was a story riddled with abuse and hardship. The couple grew to love this woman. Eventually they learned that she didn't have a place to stay, so they invited her to live with them until they could find her a room at local charity that helped women get back on their feet. Even more amazing, this gracious gesture came after the young couple had just given birth to twin babies! Again, following Jesus isn't always convenient. The fledgling parents invited her in, even still.

This woman told her friends how the couple loved and cared for her, and soon, other women with similarly heartbreaking pasts and presents came to know this couple and began learn from them. After some time, the couple decided to start a full-time street ministry for prostitutes, sex trafficking survivors, and addicts. Today, they teach these young men and women how to make beautiful stationary. They teach them social and business skills. Most importantly, they teach them that Jesus loves them. Isn't that awesome? It is amazing what God can do when we are willing to "move toward the mess" and simply be the hands and feet of Jesus. (See 1 Corinthians 12)

Hambrick really pulled at my heartstrings with the humbling truth that "We're all in the mess together." This mess isn't found in a particular people group or place; it's all around us and inside each of us. According to Hambrick, "We need only to look at our own hearts, our own families, our own lives. If we decide to follow Jesus, the first mess we will encounter is our own." That is the kind of journey that we must take if we want our souls to be healthy. The journey is often inconvenient and messy, but is incredibly beautiful.

Life is messy, and Jesus didn't come to Earth to clean it all up or avoid the messes altogether. He came to love and to serve, and He gave His life for our freedom. The mess is our mission field.

A few years ago, Dave and I took our eldest son, Cooper, and visited a place where the life-changing power of love and an awe-inspiring move toward the mess was evident everywhere I looked. It's a place of profound spiritual healing that ministers to children who have experienced heartbreaking situations. It's an orphanage in Guatemala called Casa Shalom. The name means "House of Peace," and it truly is a place of peace and love for the nearly one hundred precious kids who call it home.

Our friends Josh and Jessica are investing their lives into leading this orphanage while simultaneously raising their own young family. In the midst of all this, Jessica has courageously fought and won a battle against cancer. They're a heroic couple, and undoubtedly, their ongoing legacy of love will shape countless lives for generations to come.

As Josh gave our mission team a tour of the property, he told us the story of how each child came to be there. "There goes Eduardo. His parents were killed by drug dealers. That's Rosa. She and her brothers were living on the streets before they were brought here. They were eating out of trash cans and severely malnourished."

Each child had a heartbreaking background. Despite the brokenness of their home situations, these children seemed so happy and healthy. Josh knew each one by name, and he beamed like a proud papa as he hugged the kids and bragged about how they were great at soccer or art or singing.

At one point a teenage girl walked up and gave Josh a hug, and as she skipped away, Josh had tears in his eyes. He began to tell me her story. "Her name is Margerita," he said. "She grew up in a home with horrific abuse. Her father was a drunk, and he abused her in the worst kinds of ways. She was eventually taken out of that home and placed in a home with her aunt and uncle, but her uncle abused her in the same terrible ways that her father had done. She stayed in several more homes, but in each situation, the very people who should have been protecting her abused her. When she finally came here, she was brokenhearted and alone. She didn't trust anyone. She barely spoke. We weren't sure if we'd ever get through to her. We kept praying for her and doing our best to show her God's love in meaningful ways, but after several months of trying, nothing seemed to be working."

Josh paused to wipe some tears from his eyes as he continued the story. "One night, Jessica and I were sitting on the hillside watching the sunset like we do most nights. We were watching the boys play soccer and the girls jump rope, taking in all the beautiful sights and sounds of Casa Shalom. Then, Margerita came and sat down. She had always kept her distance, especially from men, but she scooted right next to me, and what she did next completely took my breath away. She rested her head on my shoulder. I held my breath, waiting for her to speak. When she finally looked up at me, she spoke words that I will never forget."

Josh gathered his composure, and with a smile on his face, he relived that beautiful moment. "She looked up at me and said, 'When I first came here, I never believed I would ever be safe, and I never believed anyone would ever really love me. But now I know I'm safe here. And I believe that you really love me.'"

That became a life-changing moment for Josh, a beautiful picture of what love really means. The way God loves us and the way Josh and Jessica love Margerita (and every child at Casa Shalom) shows us how love is supposed to look. Jesus brought healing to Margerita's broken heart through their love and willingness to embrace her just as she was—no matter how messy her feelings or behavior or background might have been. They loved her and continue to love her today because Jesus loves her, and because they know that He loves them, too—along with all those precious kiddos at Casa Shalom.

When we experience real love, it always has the power to bring spiritual healing and transformation. As God's love takes root in our hearts, our lives and the lives of our loved ones will be dramatically changed. No matter what you've been through, Jesus has the power to bring healing to your deepest wounds.

Dave

I'm convinced that present pain can be rooted in painful events from the past. Childhood trauma can create deep scars and lasting effects. Sometimes this pain can manifest itself in peculiar ways.

When I was a kid, one of my favorite movies was *Back to the Future*. I was fascinated by the idea of traveling through time and changing history. I even spotted an old DeLorean in our neighborhood and was tempted to peek inside to see if Doc and Marty McFly were lost in time and looking for a way back to 1985. (I'm kind of a dork when it comes to my fascination with 1980s movies.)

As much as I love those movies, what I've found as I've gotten older is that traveling to the past can be good entertainment, but is a very poor way to live in real life. We do have the power to shape the future, but unless you actually own a time machine, worrying about the past is a complete waste of your energy and your time. If you want to live a life of love and enjoy the freedom it brings, you've got to make peace with your past.

We should learn from our past and build on our past but never dwell on our past. Just like the rearview mirror in your car, looking at the past gives us perspective, but if you stare at it all the time, you're going to cause a wreck. We need to embrace the moment we are in. Don't let regrets from yesterday or worries about tomorrow rob you of the peace and blessings God has for you today!

If you are one of the many who feel stuck in a rut of living in past regrets or trying to recreate past glories, here are a few principles to help you move forward:

1. Your past sins were all paid for on the cross.

Jesus took the punishment that was meant for you and me, and by faith in Him, we are totally forgiven. From the cross He said, "It is finished!" (John 19:30). He didn't say, "You'd better spend the rest of your life feeling bad about what you did." He came to this Earth to bring life and freedom, so don't beat yourself up for mistakes that He has literally already taken the beating to forgive. It's time to let go.

2. **Your past does not define you.**

It's easy to believe the lie that the things we have done and the things that have been done to us are what give us our identity. The truth is that your past has helped shape your character, but it has nothing to do with your identity. Your identity comes from God alone, and He loves you unconditionally.

3. **Your best days are ahead.**

Don't get trapped trying to recreate the good old days when your best days are still to come. Celebrate warm memories and milestones, but don't live your life in an artificial time warp. Each day, God has new blessings in store for you. Every sunrise is a reminder that our God is always creating new beginnings and new opportunities. Don't miss them by looking back.

The song that set the tone for the whole *Back to the Future* soundtrack was "The Power of Love" by Huey Lewis and the News. If there was a movie about your life, I'm convinced God would want "The Power of Love" to set the tone. It might not be the actual song—although Huey Lewis rocks—but the real power of love that God makes possible in our lives. His love has the power to bring peace to your past, freedom to your present, and hope for your future. Time does not heal all wounds; but thankfully, Jesus heals all wounds for those who trust their wounds to Him.

Like everyone else, I have wounds from the past which still can manifest themselves in the present. When I was six years old, my cousin Teana and her dad died on the same day in a boating accident. Teana was part of my family, but she was also one of my closest friends. Their deaths on the water completely rocked my young mind. More than a generation later, the ripple effects from that single tragedy continue to impact my family.

My dad took me fishing a couple weeks after the funeral. We caught a fish and then Dad filleted it with his knife. As I watched that fish being cut up, somehow my mind connected the fish's death to my cousin's death on the water. In that moment, seafood became completely unappetizing. I was repulsed by the smell of it and the taste of it. Even microwaveable fish sticks lost their luster.

All these decades later, I still don't eat seafood. I'd like to. I've tried to. Intellectually, I understand that my aversion to seafood is completely illogical and I should be able to enjoy it. Still, something happened in the hardwiring of my young mind, which has never been completely undone. I'm still as repulsed by seafood today as when the tragedy first took place.

I live with a dietary quirk that doesn't really alter the quality of my life in any significant way, but many people experience much deeper scars. Perhaps a past trauma has left you with baggage that's much more noticeable than a dislike for seafood. Maybe you've lived with real physical pain, emotional pain or relational brokenness because of things that took place decades earlier. I've been encouraged through the years by friends who have overcome unimaginable past tragedies through their faith and relentless hope.

I've seen many friends over the years who have allowed wounds from their past to shape their lives in ways much more significant than avoiding seafood. I've known people who numb their past pain by excess drinking or overindulging in food. I've known women who felt unloved as little girls who became promiscuous as young women as a cry for attention and affirmation from men. I've known men who felt powerless or unloved as boys who became obsessively driven and aggressive, willing to hurt others if it meant that they themselves never had to feel powerless again.

It seems to me that most of the present manifestations of these past wounds stem either from feeling powerless or unloved. I felt powerless when my cousin and uncle died, but I always knew I was loved by God and my family. That love gave me strength. When a child feels both powerless and unloved—often because of the abuse and/or absence of a father—that child might grow up trying in vain to numb the pain caused years ago.

"Father wounds" are some of the deepest wounds. Thankfully, I had and still have a wonderful and loving father and mother. They gave my brothers and me such a safe environment in which to grow up and a solid foundation for our futures. I know that many were not so blessed.

I believe some of the greatest world-changers are the unsung men who grew up with absent or abusive fathers, yet choose to break the generational cycle and become present and loving fathers for their own children. This also applies to the courageous women who grew up in broken home environments, and yet they make great efforts to change their family legacy by becoming loving mothers. These are real heroes.

If you are living with pain from the past, I know those scars can still feel like fresh wounds. Whether your pain is rooted in past tragedy, loss, abandonment, failure, abuse, or anything else, the cause isn't nearly as important as the solution. The solution, in short, is Jesus.

Healing begins by allowing our Savior to comfort us and remembering that our identity is defined completely by Him. We're not defined by our past pains, our past failures, or even our past successes. We're defined by the fact that the God of the universe loves us and has adopted us into His eternal family, as a result of His grace and our faith in Him. The more we stay connected to

Him—as the branch must stay connected to the vine—the more His healing can sustain and heal us.

We'll experience this connection when we make our daily walk with Him a priority through prayer, reading the Bible and pursuing hope and growth, like you're doing right now as you read this book. We also experience His healing through healthy relationships with other people and by using our God-given gifts and skills to serve others. God's plan for healing is always rooted in relationships, both relationships with Him and with others. Don't try to do it alone. I know you've been hurt deeply, but you are loved even more deeply.

Ashley

The need for spiritual healing is often rooted in the need to forgive. Many of us are carrying around old wounds because of wrongs we haven't forgiven in others or perhaps wrongs we haven't forgiven in ourselves. Until we can truly embrace God's grace and start seeing ourselves and others through His eyes, we'll stay stuck in a cycle of damaging decisions and fractured self-worth.

One of the most popular TV movies around a decade ago was Lifetime's *The Client List*, which chronicled the true story of a Texas wife and mom who started making income as a prostitute under the guise of a massage therapist. (The film eventually became a full series.) Her double life was finally brought to light when the massage parlor/brothel was raided by police and her secrets were exposed. Her husband was disgusted and shocked, and she was eventually abandoned by everyone she loved.

You might think that kind of provocative storyline only happens on TV, but the Bible actually has a similar story—but with a much better ending! The Bible's version is about a man named Hosea and his wife, Gomer. Hosea loved his wife unconditionally, but that was put to the test when she abandoned her husband and family to return to her old life of prostitution.

By the time Hosea found out, they'd had several children, and he wasn't sure if any of them were biologically his. To make matters even worse, her crimes had landed her in prison, and based on the laws of the day, her next step was to be sold into slavery to repay her debts. Gomer's future—and their future together as a couple—was bleak. Hosea had every earthly right to write her off and leave her to the fate she had created for herself, but God had a different plan. God wanted to use this whole situation to show the amazing grace and unimaginable love He has for us, even in those moments when we are completely unworthy.

God moved Hosea's heart toward forgiveness and compassion. Hosea went to that slave auction and used most his life's savings to purchase back his wife. Based on the culture's legal system, Gomer then would have had no rights at all. Hosea would have had all the power in the relationship, and he could have used it to punish her for the rest of her life. Knowing this, she bowed her head to him and called him, "Master."

What happened next is one of the most beautiful displays of grace ever recorded. In essence, Hosea looked at her and said, "Never call me your master. I am your husband." "He gave up his right to punish, control or humiliate her. Instead, he welcomed Gomer home as his wife. This simple but powerful act of forgiveness shows us a beautiful picture of the unmerited grace and love God offers to us all. How amazing is His love for us? It's unfathomable! I love how Paul puts it when he is writing to the Ephesians. He says, "And may you have the power to understand, as all God's people should, how wide, how long, how high, and how deep his love is. May you experience the love of Christ, though it is too great to understand fully. Then you will be made complete with all the fullness of life and power that comes from God" (Ephesians 3:18-19).

I'm not sure how trust has been broken in your marriage and other relationships, and I'm definitely not advocating that you give your loved ones a free pass to break your heart. A healthy relationship must be built on trust, accountability, and mutual respect. My hope is simply that this story will open your mind and your heart a little wider to let more love and grace flow into your life.

If we deserved forgiveness, it wouldn't be called grace. If we could earn it, it wouldn't be real love. That type of radical forgiveness doesn't seem humanly possible, but it is possible through the grace Christ has extended to each of us. Forgiveness sets you free and makes healing possible in the relationship.

Some couples get stuck in a cycle of grudges and mistrust, because they wrongly assume that forgiveness and trust are the same thing. It's vital that we understand their distinctions. Forgiveness can't be earned; it can only be given freely. That's why it's called grace. Trust, however, can't be given freely; it can only be earned.

When your spouse breaks your trust, you should offer your forgiveness instantly but give your trust slowly, as trust is earned through consistency of actions. During this period of rebuilding, fight the urge to punish or retaliate. Those actions won't do anything to promote healing. Healing always needs to be our ultimate objective.

You don't have to trust someone in order to forgive, but you do have to forgive someone in order for trust to be possible again. The process of rebuilding trust might be slow and it might be painful, but it's worth it! Once you've worked through your issues and reestablished trust, your relationship can actually become stronger and more vibrant than it ever was before. Friend, please stop holding grudges! Put down the poison. Free yourself from that trap, and watch how God will heal your heart, your relationship with Him, and your marriage and family.

Have the courage to forgive your spouse today. Have the courage to forgive yourself. Have the courage to say you are sorry. Be ready and willing to do whatever it takes to rebuild the trust in your relationship. Jesus has already paid the price for your sin. Jesus's blood is enough for you. You are precious in His eyes. Embrace His grace and extend that grace to others, and you'll be taking a huge step toward spiritual healing and true freedom.

Dave

There are many stories in history of unlikely heroes who have stepped into their moments of destiny to bring immeasurable impact, spiritual healing, and social change. Most of these people weren't looking for notoriety. They were simply willing to do the right thing when it mattered most. One such hero is a first-century monk named Telemachus.[2]

Telemachus lived during the reign of the Roman Empire. During his lifetime, Christianity was spreading rapidly, but the kingdom Christ preached seemed to conflict with the empire Rome was trying to build. Roman leaders were threatened by those who would follow a carpenter king with more loyalty than they'd follow Caesar.

It was a time of great violence and turmoil. Rome enforced its power with brutal force, and any enemies or perceived enemies of the empire were killed in gruesome and public ways. The public executions and crucifixions were meant to be a deterrent to those who would challenge Roman rule and supremacy. The most

2. John Huffman et al., "Telemachus: One Man Empties the Roman Coliseum," Discerning History, July 18, 2017, http://discerninghistory.com/2016/09/telemachus-one-man-empties-the-roman-coliseum/.

famous example of gratuitous violence and death took place in the Roman Colosseum where gladiators would fight to the death for the entertainment of the masses.

The gladiator games fed the bloodlust of the people. Otherwise mild-mannered citizens would become drunk on the violence and spectacle of the gladiator games. The Colosseum was packed daily to watch prisoners and persecuted Christians being chased and eaten alive by hungry lions, or to watch gladiators fight to the death. Some gladiators were considered to be a form of professional athletes, but most of these so-called gladiators were prisoners who were forced to fight to the death, in the hopes of one day earning their freedom.

The gladiator games were a sick game with no winners. Those who performed in the arena never truly won, because they were essentially slaves to a broken system from which they could rarely escape. The spectators never won, because even though they felt entertained by the momentarily thrill of the battle, the dehumanizing violence almost certainly had negative impacts on their daily lives and experiences.

At the height of the gladiator games' popularity, an unassuming Christian monk named Telemachus was making his first visit to the big city of Rome. He wasn't sure what to expect because he hailed from a rural setting. His life had been a simple one of prayer and service to others, but he felt compelled by God to visit the busy metropolis of Rome.

Telemachus stepped off the boat in the Roman port, and I would bet his eyes widened as he processed all the sights, sounds and smells of the big city. He'd never seen anything like it before. As he tried to get his bearings in the large city, he quickly found himself being swept up into the current of a moving crowd. Thousands of people were rushing into the Colosseum, and Telemachus followed the crowd into the huge stadium.

Not knowing what to expect, he looked around and saw raving fans screaming and clapping at the dusty ground at the center of the arena. Telemachus turned his eyes to the center of the stadium and was shocked to see men battling to the death. With every clang of the sword, with every spilling of blood and with every kill, the crowd became enraptured with enthusiasm. Telemachus was shocked at the depravity and inhumanity he saw all around him.

The monk began trying to appeal to the people around him, but no one would listen to him. They were so engrossed in the battle, so Telemachus realized the only way to bring any change would be to put himself on the field of battle. Throwing caution to the wind, the monk rushed to the wall separating the seats from the field of battle and hurled himself over. He was now unarmed and completely vulnerable.

Telemachus began running to gladiators as they fought and pleading with them to stop. He fearlessly shouted, "In the name of the Lord Jesus Christ, King of Kings and Lord of Lords, I command these wicked games to cease. Do not requite God's mercy by shedding innocent blood."

The gladiators probably assumed he was a drunk spectator, and they tossed him aside. Telemachus persisted and his presence on the field of battle went from an entertaining sideshow to an annoying nuisance in the eyes of the spectators. In their lust for more blood, the spectators began shouting, "Kill him! Kill him!"

Fueled by public pressure, one of the gladiators took his sword and ran it through the torso of the unarmed monk. Telemachus fell to his knees in the middle of the Colosseum. It was the place in the stadium where the acoustics were best, so for the first time, the entire crowd could hear what the man had been shouting all along. With his dying breaths, he shouted once more, "In the name of Christ, stop this."

As Telemachus died in the center of that bloody arena, the cheering stopped, and a silence swept over the crowd. The gladiators stopped fighting, unsure what to do next. One by one, spectators began leaving the stadium in a solemn silence. Haunted and convicted by what they'd just seen, their collective conscience had been seared.

In one single act of courage, a simple man of faith had turned the tide of public opinion on one of the most brutal (and popular) traditions of the ancient world. He had also pointed the pagan crowd toward the hope that is found in Christ alone. Telemachus didn't just tweet about the problem or complain about the problem; he had the courage to take action, and history changed as a result.

A generation later, Rome would be a very different place. The gladiator games had ended for good and Christianity had gone from a persecuted religion to the official religion of the empire. There were, of course, many factors at play that made these changes a reality, but I'm convinced the courage and self-sacrifice of Telemachus and other unsung heroes like him were a huge part of turning the tide.

Like Telemachus, we need to have the courage to step into battle and say, "In the name of Christ, stop this!" We must be able to stand against popular public opinion and stand against those who would exploit others. We must courageously stand in the gap for those who are hurting and use our influence to stand against evil and stand for spiritual healing.

Look for ways to partner with your spouse to be a force of good in the world. Part of why God brought you and your spouse together is to help promote spiritual healing in each other. But He also brought you together to be partners on mission in the world to be the hands and feet of Jesus.

So, what next steps toward spiritual healing do you need to take personally? Are you having trouble letting go of a grudge? Let today be the day that you leave it at the feet of Jesus and let it go. Justice belongs to Him. Let His freedom and love reign in your life. If you are struggling with accepting His love as your own, start praying that He would help you to see yourself as He sees you—His masterpiece, His Son or His Daughter, and His beloved. If you don't quite know Jesus yet, start reading the Bible. I encourage you to begin with the four Gospels (Matthew, Mark, Luke, and John) in the New Testament. He died for you and loves you so much! He wants you to be spiritually healthy, and that starts with having a relationship with Him.

What steps can you and your spouse take together to foster spiritual healing in your marriage? If you aren't currently praying together, I encourage you to start making that a new daily habit. You don't have to say the perfect words or be a biblical theologian; just talk to God like He is your loving Father, because that is exactly who He is. Tell Him what's on your heart. Thank Him for all He has done in your lives, seek His forgiveness for any wrongdoings. Ask Him for what you need, and be willing to follow Him where He leads you. I truly believe that this one step has the power to completely transform your marriage, and it will go a long way toward improving your spiritual health and spiritual healing as a couple.

Be advocates for your own spiritual healing and for your spouse's as well, but don't stop there. Begin praying about opportunities in your community—and in the world around you—for you and your spouse to step onto the proverbial battlefield to fight the good fight for others' healing and freedom. God doesn't just want your life to be better as a result of your marriage; He wants the world to be a better place through the legacy of your marriage.

CHAPTER 10:

Finishing Strong

Ashley

When I think about the ultimate test of love, my mind goes back to a story I first learned in Sunday school when I was a small child. This test of love and faith made a profound impression on my young mind. It's also a profound example of what it means to finish strong.

In Genesis 21, we learn that Abraham was an old man enjoying the twilight years with his wife, Sarah. They had been unable to have children, and due to their advanced ages, the dream for a family had died many decades earlier. Their lives and their marriage had not (yet) turned out the way they'd dreamed. As a mother, I can imagine how heartbreaking this must have been for Sarah. Her lifelong yearning to be a mother had gone unfulfilled for so long that I'm sure she had tried to forget that dream. However, no matter how hard she tried, she couldn't shake it.

But in the midst of their elder years, God promised Abraham and Sarah that they would have a child. Sarah laughed out loud at the idea. On the surface, it did seem pretty ridiculous. She was probably thinking, "I'm going to be the only person at Walmart buying diapers for my baby *and* diapers for my husband and me at the same time!"

God has a great sense of humor. Since he invented laughter, I suppose we shouldn't be surprised that He also creates plenty of scenarios that induce laughter. True to His promise, God gave Abraham and Sarah a son. The only logical name for the boy was Isaac, because the name literally means "laughter." Isn't that just the sweetest?

Isaac was the apple of Abraham's eye. He was tangible proof of God's faithfulness. He embodied the promise of the great nation that God would birth through Abraham's lineage. He was the first in a line of descendants that would someday rival the stars in the sky in number.

Isaac was Abraham's whole life. For that reason, Isaac became the perfect test. God told Abraham to take Isaac up the mountain where he was to build an altar and sacrifice his son. Abraham was commanded to kill Isaac.

On the surface, this test may seem barbaric and cruel, but once you see how it plays out, you might have a different perspective. Obedience to God's commands always brings blessings, not only for ourselves but also for the glory of God. This situation would prove to be no different.

As you can imagine, Abraham was heartbroken at even the thought of carrying out this task. He loved his son more than life. I'm sure his head was spinning in a thousand different directions as he tried to make sense of this seemingly incomprehensible mission from a loving God. Abraham finally came to the place where he decided faith doesn't mean having everything figured out. Faith is a choice, not a feeling. Faith means choosing to trust God even when life doesn't seem to make sense. And, this certainly didn't make sense at all.

Abraham told Isaac that they needed to load up their donkey and make a trip up the mountain to give a sacrifice to God. In their era, it wasn't uncommon to make burnt offerings to God with slaughtered animals, but in this case, they were making the trip up the mountain without a suitable animal. Isaac kept asking his father about this logistical oversight, and Abraham would answer cryptically, "My son, the Lord Himself will provide the sacrifice."

They made it up the mountain, and once the altar was built, Abraham picked up his young son and placed him on it. I've often wondered what was going through Abraham's and Isaac's minds during this defining moment. I'm sure both their lives flashed before their eyes as Abraham raised the knife. What happened next was extraordinary. I want you to hear this next part straight from the source:

> *At that moment the angel of the LORD called to him from heaven, "Abraham! Abraham!"*
> *"Yes," Abraham replied. "Here I am!"*
> *"Don't lay a hand on the boy!" the angel said. "Do not hurt him in any way, for now I know that you truly fear God. You have not withheld from me even your son, your only son."*
> (Genesis 22:11–12 NLT)

It had all been a test. Abraham had shown he was willing to make the ultimate sacrifice out of love and obedience to God. The test, however, wasn't only for Abraham. It was masterfully written into God's unfolding story of grace to foreshadow the greatest act of love the world would ever know.

Centuries later, God would make the ultimate sacrifice on our behalf. He would place *His* only son on an altar. The altar would be in the shape of a cross.

Isaac was rescued at the last moment, but Jesus was not. Jesus could have called down an army of angels to rescue him, but love compelled him to stay. The father and the son followed through on the ultimate sacrifice, motivated by love for you and for me. God never intended for Abraham to sacrifice his son, but it was a price that God Himself was prepared to pay to ransom humanity from the penalty of sin. Jesus completing His mission on the cross is the ultimate example of what it means to "finish strong," and He did it motivated by His amazing love for us.

Dave

David Goggins is a retired Navy SEAL and an ultra endurance athlete who has broken Guinness World Records for his amazing feats of physical discipline. In his bestselling book, *Can't Hurt Me*, he recounts his harrowing story of overcoming a childhood where he continually endured racism, poverty, physical abuse and learning disabilities. As a young man, he also struggled with obesity.

By his own account, his life was directionless and out of control. He eventually dedicated himself to the seemingly impossible goal of becoming a Navy SEAL, which requires the most grueling mental and physical training in all of the military. Everything he did was fixated on reaching this one goal. In the process, he transformed his mind and body and he went from simply surviving into a man living with purpose. Today he challenges others to do the same. One quote from his book that resonated with me and challenged me was this: "You are in danger of living a life so comfortable and soft that you will die without ever realizing your true potential." Mic drop.

Perhaps you don't have a goal to become a Navy SEAL or record-breaking endurance athlete, but I want to give you a challenge that could be even more important than those great endeavors. I want to challenge you to become the best spouse you can possibly be. Imagine how your marriage could transform if you worked as hard on your marriage as David Goggins worked on his physical conditioning.

Perhaps the dream of having a wonderful marriage seems as impossible as becoming a SEAL seemed to Goggins when he was out of shape and directionless. Maybe your marriage is already good, but you know it could be better and you don't want to settle for "good enough" when "great" is within reach with some work. Your marriage is always worth the effort! If you'll make your marriage a priority and then relentlessly work toward self-improvement, serving your spouse, making faith a priority through prayer and reading the Word, and being as present as possible, your marriage will grow and thrive.

One of Goggins's most inspiring life principles is what he calls the "40 Percent Rule." He said that in his own life and physical training he's learned that when you reach that moment of exhaustion—when you feel completely spent and you can't go another step—you're actually only 40 percent of the way to your limit. Once you push through those moments of discomfort and keep your eyes on the prize, you'll be amazed at how much further you can actually go.

I believe this 40 Percent Rule can apply to marriage, too. We have seen so many couples reach a point where one or both spouses reach their limit. Feeling tired or frustrated, they wave the metaphorical white flag of surrender and file for divorce, never realizing that their marriage breakthrough might have been just around the corner if they had kept going. Maybe when they thought they couldn't go another step; they were actually only 40 percent spent. Had they pushed through the discomfort and kept fighting for the marriage, it could have ended in healing instead of divorce.

We are *not* endorsing this rule to keep people trapped in abusive situations. You should never be forced to endure abuse in your marriage. If you feel physically unsafe, you need to get out and get help right away.

We *are* challenging those of you who are simply frustrated. You're tired. You feel like you've given all you can give. Don't give up! Your marriage is worth it, and you are much stronger than you think.

As followers of Christ, we also have a "super fuel" in the tank that David Goggins never mentions in his book. He talks only of physical and mental strength, which alone are never enough to make a marriage thrive. (Sadly, this is perhaps why both of his marriages have ended in divorce.) While he has achieved incredible feats of endurance using only his own strength, willpower and grit, we as Christians have a spiritual power much greater than ourselves. Even when we reach the 100 percent capacity, we're comforted in knowing that the Holy Spirit is fighting our battles for us once we've invited the Lord to lead our lives and our families.

There's another reason spiritual strength is just as important (and possibly more important) to your marriage than your own physical and emotional effort. It is that your own grit and determination alone, without constant connection to Christ, can lead to a calloused heart. When you're running hard and working out, callouses on your feet and hands can actually make you stronger. But a calloused heart can only make you weaker by causing coldness and bitterness to take the place of humility, tenderness and compassion. Yes, we need to work hard at marriage, but we can't let our effort turn into pride and bitterness. We must allow the

Holy Spirit to do His work in us and through us, so our hearts stay in the right posture to give and receive love.

The Bible tells us that our battle isn't against flesh and blood but is a spiritual battle (Ephesians 6:12). In other words, you have a real enemy who hates your marriage and wants to see it sabotaged, but when you follow Christ, you have a real Savior who is stronger. Once you've invited Christ to be the leader of your life and your marriage, His strength in you is always stronger than any challenge you'll face. He will be with you every step of the way.

When we stay connected to Christ, we'll have the faith to persevere in the race of life (which is more important and more difficult than finishing an ultramarathon). He will give us the strength not only to start strong, but to stay strong as we continue to follow Him. I love how Paul puts this in Hebrews 12:2. *"We do this by keeping our eyes on Jesus, the champion who initiates and perfects our faith. Because of the joy awaiting him, he endured the cross, disregarding its shame. Now he is seated in the place of honor beside God's throne"* (NLT).

Ashley

Finishing strong in any part of life comes down to the habits we choose to implement consistently. Things we do once or twice rarely change our lives, but those things we do faithfully every day can be a powerful force. Dave and I were reminded of this when we met an extraordinary couple named Harold and Louise at one of our marriage events. There was a sparkle in their eyes and an adoration they obviously had for one another. They couldn't help but smile at one another every time their eyes met. Even though they were both in their seventies and mobility issues required Harold pushing Louise in her wheelchair, they acted like two teenagers in love. It was truly a precious sight.

Dave and I tried to spend as much time around them as we could that weekend, because we wanted to learn the "secret" of their lifelong love. We wanted to know how their love had grown richer with time and how even through painful setbacks in Louise's health, they both remained joyful, optimistic, and passionately devoted to one another.

When we asked them about the secret to their lifelong love and lasting joy, Louise's eyes lit up as she looked up at Harold. She smiled, looked back at me, cleared her throat and said, "Our first date was on March 17, so on April 17, Harold brought me a long-stem rose to celebrate our one-month anniversary. I was genuinely impressed by his thoughtfulness, but I didn't expect the roses to come very often. I was so surprised when he brought me another rose on May 17 to celebrate our second month together. I smiled and thought, 'Wow! This fella is a keeper!'"

She looked up at Harold with a smile and continued her story. "After we got married, I expected the roses to stop, but on the seventeenth that first month of our marriage, another rose appeared." She paused to squeeze Harold's hand and tears began to form in her eyes as she said, "It has been fifty-four years since our first date, and every month on the seventeenth, for 648 months in a row, Harold has brought me a rose. He hasn't missed a one!"

Harold and Louise definitely challenged Dave and me to raise the bar in our own marriage! Dave and I obviously can't build a time machine and go back to the beginning and start that type of tradition, but we can be intentional about bringing more thoughtfulness and romance into our marriage. And, you can, too!

Harold and Louise would be quick to tell you that it takes a lot more than roses to build a strong, lifelong marriage. The flowers weren't really the point of their story; it was the thoughtfulness behind the flowers. As we spend time with couples who have faithfully loved each other for decades, we're convinced that their "secret" is really no secret at all. It's a simple choice to put love into action by consistently serving, encouraging, supporting and adoring one another.

As we prepare to wrap up this this book, we encourage you to think about one or two new habits you'd like to implement into your life and marriage, then one or two negative habits you'll take action to remove from your life and marriage. Your habits will shape your life, so make sure you're choosing the right ones. Eliminating a few unhealthy habits and implementing one or two new, healthy habits could make a life-changing difference for you and your spouse and family.

Please don't toss this book aside until you've committed to some *new* habits. Be specific and hold yourself accountable to it. Your habits are the keys to your health.

Dave

I'm so glad Ashley shared that story about Harold and Louise! She used to tease me about how often I would tell that story at our marriage events, but I know that she loves their story as much as I do! I've got another story for you, and this one is probably one you've heard before. It's from one of my favorite movies.

The Academy Award–winning World War II movie *Saving Private Ryan* tells the story of a young soldier (Private Ryan) whose brothers had been killed in battle. To spare his family the agony of losing all of their sons, the government orchestrated a rescue mission to save him and send him home. The rescue team was led by a no-nonsense Army captain who seemed to believe that the whole thing was a bad idea.

In the film's final scene, the captain is fatally wounded while fulfilling his mission. With his dying words, he looks Private Ryan in the eyes and says, "Earn this! Earn it." The end of the movie skips forward many decades and we see Private Ryan as an old man standing at the grave of that captain. You can tell he has been haunted by those words and trying to "earn it" all of his life, but he never knows for sure if he has measured up. He pleads with the grave, seeking approval, but he finds none.

Many people believe they have put their faith in Jesus, but they also believe they have to earn what He did for them on the cross. Here's the good news: when Jesus was hanging on that cross, dying to save you, He did not use his final words to say, "Earn this." Do you know what He said instead? He said, "It is finished!" (John 19:30).

Did you catch that? It is finished! That means done, complete, sealed, finished! That's God's gift of grace. Jesus has done *all* the work already. You couldn't possibly earn it, even if you tried with everything you had. God never expected you to earn it.

The Bible says that if you confess that Jesus is Lord and believe in your heart that God raised him from the dead, then you will be saved (Romans 10:9). It's not something you have to earn; it's a gift for you to receive by faith. Reach out to your Savior and love God with your whole heart, mind, soul, and strength. He's already done all the work, and He did it out of love for you. It is finished.

Yes, finishing strong requires faith and work and effort on our part. We must put in the time to have optimum mental health, physical health, spiritual health, and overall marriage health. Our effort matters, but our salvation is a gift, and Jesus has already done all the work. We can't finish strong until we've put our faith and trust in Him.

If you haven't asked Jesus to be the leader of your life and the forgiver of your sins, ask Him today. If you haven't asked Him to be the one to lead your marriage and bring healing to what's wounded in your heart, ask Him today. If you haven't asked Jesus to guide your steps toward all He has in store for you, ask today. His plans for your life are healthier and better than anything you could imagine.

Don't settle for less than the life He has for you. He is with you in this journey (Joshua 1:9). He is for you (Philippians 4:13). He will never leave you or forsake you (Hebrews 13:5).

Ashley

I love that powerful example from *Saving Private Ryan*, but we have found that real-life stories can be even more powerful than any script from Hollywood. Our friend, Jamey, is a police officer in Georgia, and recently had to report to a home where a woman had just died of natural causes. As he made his way into the house, he saw a frail, elderly man weeping by the bed where his beloved wife lay. Jamey was moved by the tenderness, devotion, and love that had obviously held this marriage together for so many years.

After the coroner came, Jamey had the opportunity to sit down with the grieving husband to hear some wonderful stories. A surge of youthful energy flooded the old man's voice as he described their teenage marriage and how they'd run off to the West Coast with only pennies in their pockets to start their new life together. The sparkle in his eyes was undeniable as he relived their lifetime of love and adventure.

The elderly man talked about some of the good times and bad times and how their commitment to each other, their faith, and family had kept them grounded through all the storms. Their friendship had grown throughout their lives as they became companions, confidants, and collaborators through every season of their epic journey. Even as their health faded, their love grew. They shared so much laughter and love, and even in their hard times, they made sure there was always joy and fun.

When it came time for Jamey to leave, the old man shared one last thought that will forever stick out in our minds. He said, "Sixty-six years together...it wasn't nearly enough time. There was so much time I wasted that I wish I could go back and give to her and spend with her. It just wasn't nearly enough time together."

A good lesson for all of us to learn and remember is to cherish our time. Even in the little, everyday routines of life, try to be fully present in the moments together. Be willing to turn off the phones and screens and distractions. Make time for each other. When you look back on your life, your faith and your family will be all that matters, so please don't wait until the end of your life to make them your top priority! Your love will be the only part of your legacy that can last into eternity.

Make a deliberate decision right now to stop wasting time and start putting first things first. Give the very best of yourself to your loved ones—not the leftovers after you've given your best to everyone and everything else.

So many people wait until they're at the end of life before they discover what matters most. They enter into eternity having squandered their time on earth. That's a tragedy we want to help you avoid at all costs!

Life is short, but eternity is long. Make the most of every moment you have on earth.

"Teach us to number our days, that we may gain a heart of wisdom" (Psalm 90:12).

Here are some ways to make the most of every moment, so when that time comes, you can face it with no regrets:

1. **Be quick to forgive and to seek forgiveness.**
Life's too short to hold grudges and keep a tally of each other's faults. Let grace flow freely. It will lift a huge weight off your shoulders and theirs.

2. **Don't take each other for granted.**
Recognize that every minute together is a gift, so treasure it. Don't prioritize your hobby, your career, or your possessions over your marriage and family. In the end, your relationships will be all that matters, so don't wait to make them your priority.

3. **Laugh more.**
This one is my personal favorite! Don't take yourselves too seriously, but don't take your commitments too lightly. Live life with conviction and purpose but make plenty of room for fun. Laughter should be the soundtrack of your relationship.

4. **Don't hit the snooze button on your dreams.**
If you and your family have dreams, don't keep putting them off until "someday" gets here, because someday may never come unless you try to make it happen.

5. **Realize that most of the stuff you fight about isn't worth fighting over.**
Fight for each other, but never fight against each other. In every disagreement, remember that your relationship is much more important than whatever you're arguing about.

6. **Remember that romance has no expiration date.**

So many marriages start out strong and then slowly fade until there's nothing left, but it's not supposed to be that way. Through all the seasons of your life, continue to pursue each other, love each other, encourage each other, and treasure every moment together. If you've already fallen out of those habits, start today and begin again.

7. **Realize that goodbye doesn't have to be the end.**

Love was created to last forever. Jesus promises the hope of eternal life and eternal love (John 3:16). Because of him, *goodbye* is never the last word. That same hope can be yours, and I can tell you from experience that it truly changes everything.

Dave

One of the central teachings of the Bible is that God wants an eternal relationship with us that transcends our mortal limitations. This is made possible because God gives us a spiritual heart transplant. I grew up in church learning this kind of terminology, but it honestly never made sense until I heard this story.

In my hometown, there was a young man named Paul. I never knew Paul personally, but I was in the same grade as one of his younger sisters. One night, Paul's parents received the kind of phone call that every parent dreads—their son had been in a terrible car accident. They rushed to the hospital, and when they arrived, their worst fears were confirmed. Paul had been killed. In an instant, life as they knew it had ended.

In that moment of tragedy and devastating pain, Paul's parents were forced to make the very difficult decision of whether or not to donate their son's organs. They decided that he would have wanted to save lives through his death, so with broken hearts, they signed the papers and began the process of grieving this unimaginable loss.

After some time had passed, they decided they wanted to visit every person who had received the life-saving gift of one of Paul's organs. The hospital contacted the recipients, and each was eager to thank them in person. The parents set out on a road trip to meet these people whose lives had been changed through their son.

Each encounter was heartwarming. They met a woman who had received one of Paul's kidneys, and she hugged them and thanked them and said that she would see her children grow up because of their son's sacrifice. They met a man who had received their son's liver, and he hugged them and cried and talked about the new life that their son had given to him.

They waited to visit the man who had received their son's heart last.

As they pulled up the gravel drive, they saw him come out of his house to welcome them, and before the car came to a complete stop, Paul's mom had flung open the car door and raced to meet the man who had received her son's heart. He stood in bewilderment as she threw her arms around him and squeezed him so tightly that he could barely breathe. After a few moments of awkward silence, he tried to introduce himself, but she immediately stopped him and said, "Shhhh. Please don't speak."

She finally pulled away just far enough for him to see the tears streaming down her face. She smiled, and with a trembling voice she looked into his eyes and said, "When I hold you close to me, I can feel my son's heart beating inside of you."

One day, you and I are going to pass from this life into eternity just like Paul did. In that moment, the money you made, the fame you achieved, and the outward success you experienced will seem very insignificant. In that moment, I believe God will rush to meet you with an embrace. The arms that created the universe will wrap themselves around you, and all God will want to say to you in that moment will is this:

"When I hold you close to me, I can feel my Son's heart, the heart of Jesus, a heart of love, beating inside of you!"

When we choose to love people the way Jesus loves people, the world will change. Don't treat others the way they treat you; treat others the way that God treats you. Embrace the love of Jesus in your own life, and then model the example of Jesus in your marriage and family. Jesus changed the world with love, and He wants you and me to continue in this. He wants to give you a new heart and a new life. He wants you and your spouse to have minds, bodies, and souls that are holy, healthy, and happy.

When you step from this life into eternity, love will be all that matters. Live your life with a heart of love. Live *naked and healthy*. Live free. Live for Jesus. You'll be amazed at what will happen in your life and marriage as a result.

ACKNOWLEDGMENTS

There are so many people who have impacted our own story and also have helped give life to this book. Before we list out some important friends, colleagues and mentors who have shaped *Naked and Healthy*, we want to thank YOU for taking the time to read this book. By reading, applying, and sharing the message of this book, you've partnered with us in this work of building healthier lives and healthier marriages. Thank you!

Our deepest gratitude and appreciation goes to XO Marriage CEO, Brent Evans, who first envisioned the concept of *Naked and Healthy* and encouraged us to write it. His leadership and ongoing support makes all of our effort at XO possible. We are truly honored to call the entire Evans Family our friends and we're equally honored that they've adopted us into the *XO Marriage* family.

We are also deeply humbled and grateful to work alongside an incredible staff team and marriage coaches at *XO Marriage*. This book may have our names on the front, but like every aspect of this ministry, it was truly a team effort. We have the privilege of serving as part of a world-class team of people who serve and lead wholeheartedly with authentic faith, tenacious grit and contagious enthusiasm. We're sorry that all of their names couldn't fit on the front cover, but we definitely want to list them here. The current team at XO includes the following world-changers:

Jonathan Armbruster
Marcus Bowen

Rebecca de Broekert

Jason Boyett (this book's Editor)

Shannon Chatham

Mark and Grace Driscoll

Josey Edwards

Brent Evans

Jimmy Evans

Karen Evans

Natalie Grantham

Andrew Grekoff

Layci Jones

Karina Lopez (this book's Project Manager)

Micah Lynch

Shawn and Martita Lynch

Madison Martinez

Shelly Millheim

Victor Ortiz

Jackie Powell

Victor Da Silva

Hailey Rojas

Luis and Kristen Roman

Aliya Scott

Joni Smith

Pam Southers

Chris Stetson

Barbara Stockler

Janet Tatum

Teresa Thomas

Susan Walton

Reed Lovell (audio engineer of WestSide Studios)

We are also eternally grateful for the love and support of our family. We want to thank our parents, Brad and Karen Willis and Bill and Mary McCray for your lifelong love and support. We also want to thank our siblings and our extended family for all you do for us. Special thanks to our precious sons Cooper, Connor, Chandler and Chatham. We love you boys and all we do we do for you. The greatest honor in our lives is the privilege of being your parents.

We extend our heartfelt gratitude to our church family at Stevens Creek Church in Augusta, GA. The staff, the people and our small group at "The Creek" have been a constant source of encouragement and support for our family in ways we could never repay. We love our church!

Special thanks to our dear friends and ministry partners Gary and Susan ("Church Grammy") Youtsey and Israel and Hollie Bernal. These two extraordinary couples have encouraged us, prayed for us, adopted us into their own families and supported the ministries of *XO Marriage* in world-changing ways. We are inspired by their authentic faith, their generous spirits and their ongoing partnership in the ministry of building stronger marriages.

We also want to express our appreciation for the world's best babysitter, Cara Griffith, who has become an adopted part of our family and she loves our kids like her own when we're traveling for ministry events. Her ongoing positive impact in our kids' lives has been such a gift.

Our heartfelt gratitude also extends to our friends near and far who have helped shape the content of this book through your stories, your encouragement, and your prayers. For those social media friends and *Naked Marriage Podcast* listeners who we've never met in person but who have encouraged us, prayed for us, and shared our content with others, please know that your impact in this ministry and in our lives is profound. Thank you for your partnership in this work of building healthier marriages and pointing more people to God's love, grace, and peace.

Finally, and most importantly, we want to thank Jesus Christ, our Lord and Savior. He is the giver of all good things. True health in life, in faith, and in marriage is only possible because of Him.

ABOUT DAVE AND ASHLEY

Dave and Ashley Willis spent thirteen years in full-time church ministry before joining the XO Marriage team to build stronger, Christ-centered marriages. With XO Marriage—the largest marriage-focused ministry in the world—their books, blogs, podcasts, speaking events, and media resources have reached millions of couples worldwide. Dave and Ashley speak at all XO events, host *The Naked Marriage Podcast* and regularly create new marriage resources. They also co-host the MarriageToday broadcast on Daystar Television Network, which features their teachings alongside Founder and President of XO Marriage, Jimmy Evans.

The Willis family includes four sons from preschool to high school age, plus a rescue dog named "Chi-Chi." When Dave and Ashley aren't writing and speaking, they treasure hanging out with their family, watching movies, and taking long walks together to develop new, marriage ministry content ideas.

the
NAKED MARRIAGE

with **Dave & Ashley Willis**

REAL TESTIMONIES FROM *THE NAKED MARRIAGE PODCAST* LISTENERS

"My husband found this podcast and told me that I ought to give it a try. We thought we had a good marriage, but now that we've been listening to Dave and Ashley for a while and are practically applying what we're learning, we know it's a great marriage. We were doing things that damaged our relationship and intimacy that we didn't even realize. We are closer than ever, and we talk about Dave and Ashley all the time. My husband says they're like our really close friends, only they've never met us. Lol! Thanks Dave and Ashley!!"

—SarahAdam17

"Love this podcast! My husband and I both enjoy listening to Dave and Ashley speak wisdom into our marriage. They are so real and honest in each episode; it is so easy to relate to. We have read the book as well and it has helped us tremendously. I would 100% recommend this podcast to every marriage couple!"

—StephJewell

"I stumbled across this podcast this week after having a heart to heart with my spouse. We are great but slowly drifted from a married couple to friends and forgot to nurture our marriage. 14 years and two children and lack of communication is what hurt us. I've been reading books and listening, and this podcast is amazing. It feels like you are speaking directly to me. Thank you."

—Bgwks

"My significant other and myself listen to your podcast when we take road trips. Your podcast helps us with providing tools for our relationship toolbox. We are preparing to be married sometime in the near future and believe your book and podcast help us be in a better Christian based relationship."

—Dschall

"This podcast has given me a whole new mindset on my marriage. God has spoken to me in so many ways and I have learned so much. My heart feels gentler, I have more patience, more empathy for my husband which has made us both happier. I can't recommend this podcast enough, thank you!"

—MarGods

"You need to be listening to this with your spouse. It will help so much...and sometimes it will be pretty spicy...and there's nothing more fun than spicy with your spouse!"

—StealthSuitStanley

Learn From The Best

Hundreds of classes and videos to help

you grow closer to your spouse.

Unlimited access to leading marriage

experts, for only $9/month.